Kids Need to Know: How Kids Can Own a Business and School Won't Teach Them

Recommended for ages 3-22

Part I

Anthony Leandre Warren

Kids Need to Know , How kids can own a business and school won't teach them

Written by
Anthony Leandre Warren

Published by
Anthony Leandre Warren

I did not recieve a bachelor's degree or master's degree in writing the English language. Therefore there may be spelling, punctuation and grammatical errors. After I completed the three month process of hand writing this book, I sent it off three times to three different editors. The first two editors basically took my money and did horrible work. As I wrote in chapter 8 Building a Team. I chose bad workers even after I screened them, but I take full responsibility for the mistakes. I have never written a book nor have I put together a team to complete and publish a book. I'm saying that to say, you must move forward with FAITH, even when you don't have everything you think you need, when you are not sure things will turn out as you expect them to, when you don't know everything you think you need to know, TAKE A LEAP OF FAITH, as the saying goes. GO WITH YOUR MOVE!!

I am not a financial advisor. Everything written in this book is intended to educate the youth and others that need this information.

INTRODUCTION

Did you know that minors under the age of 18 years old can legally own a business? Yes, that is correct, but you will need the help of your parents or legal guardian.

This book was designed to develop an entrepreneurial mindset and focus before you enter the real world on your own.

To build your foundation of knowledge in business ownership, opposite to the plan of the US educational system. School was created to make good employees and excellent wage slaves. I'm here to create billion dollar business minds. In school they never tell you that you can own a business like the one you are being trained to work at.

In this book you will gain understanding of credit and how to start building it now! You will learn how to start building business credit; the difference between an asset and a liability; how to get customers for your business; how to file your LLC paperwork correctly; how to hide and protect your riches and pass them on to the next generation; over 9 different ways to gain ownership of real estate; different types of mortgage loans for entrepreneurs; how to build a team to help you succeed; and much more.

Just like building a house you start from the ground up. This is the same way you will build your business owner knowledge from the ground up. This book is your foundation and should be read often. One time is not enough to lock the information in your mind; treat this book like a Bible read!

Each chapter in this book will build that foundation you need, but after you master this book, you will need to begin growing your knowledge in each subject. This is only the beginning—let's build!

This Book was inspired by and dedicated to my babies Aulahn and Tajh. Daddy loves you.

CONTENTS

1

PERSONAL CREDIT

What is credit? Credit is the ability of a customer to obtain goods or services before payment, based on the trust that payment will be made in the future.

HOW CREDIT WORKS

Basically, credit is a deal where people or businesses give you things like money, cars, clothes, shoes, houses, jewelry, games, bikes, toys, candy and just about anything that money can buy. They give it to you first without you paying them for it. You get it now and pay it back another day.

Examples of Credit Transactions

The store that you buy your candy from. Let's say you go to the store Monday and tell the cashier to give you ice cream today and you will pay him back tomorrow.

Your best friend gives you $20 on Tuesday and you pay him or her the $20 back on Friday.

Down Payment Credit Transactions

In some cases people or businesses will ask you for a down payment when using your good credit to buy things that you want or need. A down payment is when they ask you to pay them some of the money now and pay the rest of it later.

Examples of a Down Payment

1. Let's say you want to buy a pair of Air Jordan shoes. The shoes cost $200. You would pay a down payment of $20 and take the shoes home. The other $180 that you owe for the shoes you will pay back another day.

2. A new PlayStation game has just come out and you do not have all of the money to buy it. The

game costs $100. Using your good credit you would pay a down payment of $5 and take the game home. The remaining $95 you can pay back another day.

Credit Cards

Credit cards are cards with money on them that banks, credit unions and businesses give you to buy things you need or want. Some businesses will give you credit cards that you can only use to buy items from their store like a Home Depot credit card or a Shell gas credit card. When you get a credit card from a bank or credit union you can use it to pay for just about anything that you want.

Two Types of Credit Cards

There are mainly two types of credit cards and those are secured and unsecured. With a secured credit card you will have to give them money before you get the card. With an unsecured card you do not have to give them any money before they give you the credit card.

A FEW WAYS TO START BUILDING CREDIT:

Authorized User

One fast way to start building your credit now at an early age is to ask a family member that has great credit to add you on their credit cards as an Authorized User.

Secured Credit Card

Think of a secured credit card like a pre-paid Walmart card. You will give the credit union the amount that you want to put on the card. Start small, most credit unions only require $200-$300 to receive a secured credit card. Although the method of getting the card is similar to a prepaid card, with this type of card your payments will be reported to the credit bureaus, whereas a Walmart prepaid card will not report your payments to the credit bureaus.

Ecredable

Ecredable is a company that reports your utility bill payments to the credit bureaus. You can link up to nine eligible utility account types: energy, water, gas, waste, cell phone, cable TV, satellite TV, internet and landline phone. Google search "Ecredable" and sign up.

Add Rent Payments to Your Credit Report

Just as Ecredable helps you get credit for paying bills that people normally don't get credit for there are companies that report your rent payments and history to the credit bureaus and they are: www.boompay.app, www.canrentbuildcredit .wpcomstaging.com, www.rentreporters.com, rentalkharma .com, levelcredit.com, rockthescore. com, creditrentboost .com, and paymentreport. com.

Secured Loans

Secured loans work just like secured credit cards. You will give the bank or credit union money (collateral) and they will give you a cash loan. The trick is to not spend the money they give you. Use the exact same money they gave you to pay them back. Let's say you wanted to borrow $200 from your mom or dad. You would give mom or dad your cell phone to hold as collateral, and when you pay back the $200 you get your cell phone back. But you do not spend the money, you give them the exact same $200 back that they gave you.

The 3 Credit Bureaus

A credit bureau is a company that holds your credit history and credit score. When you do not pay your bills and debt back to businesses that you owe it goes on your credit report as a bad mark and other businesses will no longer want to loan you money. When you pay your bills and money you owe to businesses on time it will also show on your credit report, but as a good mark.

Based on your credit profile for credit history you get a credit score just like in school. The personal credit score scale ranges from 300 to 850. A score of 300 would be an F in school, and a score of 850 would be an A⁺.

The 3 credit bureaus that hold your credit scores and history are Experian, Transunion and Equifax.

Pay all of your bills and people you owe money to back early! Not on time, pay them early!

BUSINESS CREDIT

WHAT IS BUSINESS CREDIT?

Business credit is your business's ability to borrow. Your business credit score influences your access to get products such as credit cards and money loans, giving credit agencies, lenders, vendors and suppliers an idea of how you handle your debts and your likelihood of paying them on time. Building your business credit will help your business a lot. The products you will be able to receive include lines of credit, business credit cards, term loans, commercial real estate loans, residential real estate loans, cars, equipment, letters of credit and more.

How Does Business Credit Work?

Business credit works like personal credit, but you will be borrowing money in the name of your business. You and your business are two separate legal entities (people). When you go to banks, credit unions and other businesses you will give them your business's information to get loans.

Personal Guarantee

Having good personal credit can help your business get the money loans, credit cards and other products from other businesses. Some lenders will require a personal guarantee from you in order for them to give loans to your business. A personal guarantee simply means you will be the co-signer for the loan, and you would be responsible for paying the loan back if your business does not.

The Business Credit Bureaus

The three business credit bureaus are Dun and Bradstreet, Experian and Equifax. These bureaus keep records and tell other businesses how your business pays back money to other businesses that you borrow money from and owe money to.

Business Credit Scores

Just like your personal credit your business will also have a credit score. The business credit score point scale is different number-wise. The business point scale ranges from 1 to 100. A score of 1 would be an F at school and a score of 100 would be an A⁺. This number is called your Paydex score.

Start Building Business Credit

A few ways to begin building your business credit is to one, apply for fuel/gas credit cards. Google search "www.waxcard.com" and apply for the gas card. Another way is to open an account with Ecredable just as you did for your personal credit. Ecredable offers business and personal credit building products and services. Google search "www.ecredable.com" and apply.

NAV Boost

Nav is a credit monitoring platform that also helps build your business's credit profile. This platform helps connect small businesses to financing options and programs. Apply with NAV and sign up for a membership—the cost of the membership will vary depending on which membership you use. By you becoming a member your monthly payments will be reported to all three of the business credit bureaus.

The Red Spectrum

Red Spectrum works similar to how NAV works. Google search www.theredspectrum.com. This company reports your membership payments to two business credit bureaus. Set up an account with them, which will cost you $99 to sign up and $49.99 per month for the business reporting services.

Credit Strong

Credit Strong is a five-star FDIC bank that has a credit building program. Log on to www.creditstrong.com and go to Credit Strong Business. When you attempt to apply you will be given two options: a 5-year plan for $199 per two months or a 10-year plan for $115 per month and you can cancel at any given time. Your monthly payments will be reported to Dun & Bradstreet and Equifax.

Credit is all about borrowing money and paying it back, as you know by now. But always remember that you pay your bills and debt back early.

BUYING A BUSINESS

WHAT IS A BUSINESS?

A business is defined as an organization for an enterprising entity engaged in commercial, industrial or professional activities. Businesses can be for-profit or non-profit organizations. The purpose of a business is to offer value to customers who pay for a product or service. Some businesses only sell products, some only provide services, and some provide services and sell products.

Product Business

A product business sells physical or virtual items. Examples of product businesses would be Foot Locker and Foot Action that sells shoes and clothes; Burger King that sells hamburgers, fries and sodas; your local AutoZone, and Advanced Auto Parts are also product selling businesses that sell car parts; jewelry stores that sell rings, watches and earrings.

Service Business

A service business is a business that performs some type of physical work for a customer like the lawn man that cuts your grass, the car wash that washes your car or truck, or the mechanic shop that repairs cars when they are broken. All of these are examples of service type businesses.

Business Structures

The most common forms of a business structure are the sole proprietorship, partnership, C-Corporation, S-Corporation and Limited Liability Company (LLC).

Franchising

If you buy a business by way of franchising, you are simply buying a business that is already established and making money. You are essentially paying to use the name of the company.

Examples of Franchising

Some examples of franchising would be buying a McDonald's, Pizza Hut, Subway, Chick-Fil-A, UPS Store, Wendy's, Jiffy Lube, Papa John's Pizza, Burger King, or Popeyes Louisiana Chicken. When choosing the franchising route of buying a business a lot of fee's come with it. Depending on which franchise you choose, you will have to buy or rent a building to do business.

The Steps in Buying a Franchise

The first step in buying a franchise will be to Google search "www.franchisedirect.com". This website will show you almost every franchise that you can buy. The second step is to scroll through all of the franchises until you find one you are interested in buying. After you choose the franchise, you want to buy go back to Google and type in the name of the franchise with the words "franchise for sale" attached to it. For example: "McDonald's franchise for sale". Once you are on the company's franchise page, they may require you to fill out a short application and wait for them to reply back to you.

Owning Businesses Through the Stock Market

The stock market is another way for you to become a business owner. In the stock market you are trading money for money, not time for money. You also do not need to spend money on all of the things that you need when building your own business or buying a franchise. That means that you do not need to hire employees, buy equipment or spend money on marketing. Your main focus when investing this way is to study the business before you buy it and knowing when to buy shares in the business.

Understanding How the Stock Market Works

When buying businesses through the stock market you can buy the whole business, or you can buy a portion of the business.

Think of the stock market like going to the mall. The mall is a market where different businesses sell products and services. Customers come to the mall (market) to buy products from those businesses.

If the mall was the stock market the businesses would be selling stocks and shares of their company to customers rather than shoes and clothes.

So instead of you going to the Apple store to buy a phone for $1,000, you would go to the store and buy $1,000 worth of shares of the company and become an owner of Apple.

Being that the mall is the stock market you could walk into every store and buy shares of their company.

STOCKS AND SHARES

Stock or stocks consist of all the shares by which ownership of a corporation or company is divided. A single share of the stock means fractional ownership of the corporation in proportion to the total number of shares.

To make it easy for you to understand we will use pizza to show you how stocks and shares work. The stock itself will be the company and shares will be slices of the pizza.

Apple (stock)

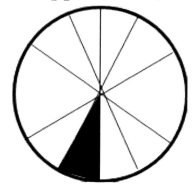

One slice of pizza
is one share, and the
cost is $10

Google (stock)

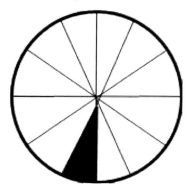

One slice of pizza
is one share, and
the cost is $15

Google (stock)

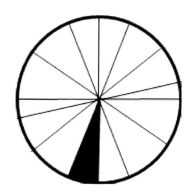

One slice of pizza is
one share, and the
cost is $20

Berkshire
Hathaway (stock)

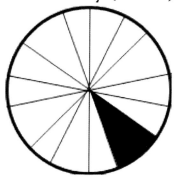

One slice of pizza
is one share, and
the cost is $100

AT+T (stock)   **Walmart (stock)**

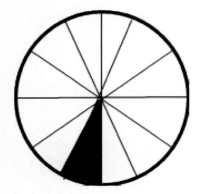 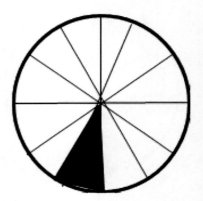

One slice of pizza is one share, and the cost is $11

One slice of pizza us one share, and the cost is $50

When buying shares in a company, every company will have a different price; some will be cheap, and some will be expensive.

How to Buy Shares

I explained to you that the mall would be the stock market and you would buy shares of companies in the mall by going to different stores inside of the mall to buy them. This was just an illustration to give you an understanding of how the stock market works. To actually buy stocks you will not have to leave your house; it is all done on the internet.

Brokerage Company

In order to buy the shares you will use a brokerage firm/ brokerage company. Two good brokerage firms are Charles Schwab and TD Ameritrade. Using the internet, go on to their website and find the section that says "Brokerage Account". As of today, you do not need any money to open the account, but you will want to put at least $20 in it as soon as possible just to keep the account open and active. The type of brokerage account you will need is a Custodial Account. So find the Custodial Account section within the Brokerage Account section on the website.

Custodial Account

To open this account you will need the help of your parent or guardian.

- Custodial Account Details

  - All assets are held in the child's name (your name)
  - A custodial account is an irrevocable gift and must be turned over to the child when he or she reaches 18 or 21, maybe even 25 years old depending on the state's laws that you live in.
  - Any funds used must be used for the benefit of the child.

Once you have this account started you should now start putting money in it regularly. Use this account like your piggy bank. The money you get for birthdays and holidays should be put in this account to start buying stocks!

How You Get Paid

Two of the ways you get paid from buying stocks is through dividends and equity.

Dividends

Dividends are the money that the business pays you when it makes money (profits). The companies that you own that pays dividends will pay you monthly, quarterly, semi-annually or annually. That means every month, every 3 months, every 6 months or once a year. Every company that pays dividends pays at different times. Some will pay you every month and others will pay you one time a year (annually).

D.R.I.P.

The word DRIP stands for Dividend Reinvestment Plan. Re-Investment means that you are putting money back into your business by buying more shares in the company that you own. You should set up a DRIP to keep your money growing. You can set this up on your account yourself.

Dividend Yield

A dividend yield is simply the percentage of the share price paid to you. Dividend yields are calculated by using the value price of the share and the dividend percentage number.

Example:

Walmart share/stock price is $150.00

Walmart dividend yield is 2.5%

What you will do is multiply 150 X .025 = $3.75 $3.75 will be your dividend payment from your Walmart shares/stock.

Being Paid in Equity

Being paid in equity means that the value of your stock/shares has increased. Your company's value has risen. Some stocks will pay you in equity and not dividends. Let's say the Walmart stock/share you bought went from $150.00 to $300.00—that's a $150.00 increase in Equity. If you wanted to you could sell the stock.

BUILDING A BUSINESS:
FILING LLC PAPERWORK

In this chapter, I will teach you how to file your Limited Liability Company (LLC) paperwork to start the process of building your own business. Before you begin the actual paperwork, you must check the Secretary of State's website to make sure nobody is using the business name that you want to use for your own business, create a domain name, business number, business email, business website and purchase a virtual address and office.

BUSINESS NAME CHECK

Google search Secretary of State in your state. Once you are on your state's S.O.S. website find the tab that says "Reserve a business name" or "Entity name check". If you have any troubles call and email the Secretary of State (S.O.S.) and ask them to walk you through this step. Tell them the name of your new business and wait for them to tell you if the name is available. This process could take up to a few days.

After you find out if the name you want for your business is available, reserve it. If it is not available, choose a new name and repeat the process.

Domain Name

A domain name is your website's equivalent of a physical address, and it helps users find your site easily. One example of a domain name is www. joeschicken.com.

Do a Google search for "google domains". Once you are on the google domains web page you should see a box that says "search for your new domain". Type the name you want in the search box and press the search button. The next page that comes up will give you a list of names to pick, such as joeschicken.net, joeschicken.org, joeschicken.info. Pick the domain you want then go to the checkout page to pay. When you get to the checkout page, you will see a box that says custom email.

You will need to get the email as well. Add a standard business email to your cart. Your business email should be formatted like this: info@joeschicken.com. Do not use a Yahoo, Gmail, AOL, or iCloud for your business email!

Your domain name will cost $12 per year and your business email will cost $12 per month. Go to the checkout and pay for both of them.

1-800 Business Number

Your business will need its own phone number that starts with 1-800, 1-888, 1-877 or 1-866. Do not use a regular city area code phone number!

RingCentral

You will use RingCentral to buy your business number; there are other companies you can use but I will be explaining to you how to set up your account with RingCentral. Google search "RingCentral", and once you are on the website's page they will ask for your name, email , phone number, company name and number of employees. You can use your personal email, personal phone number, any company name and 1-19 employees. After you type in the information press the "get a quote" button. They will send you to a different page and give you a new number. When you are on this page click the blue button that says "Change Number", then it will send you to a different page. This is the page you want.

The top of this page should say "Choose a phone number". Click the toll-free button. You will be given the option to pick an 888, 877, 866, 855, 844, 833 or 800 number. I would suggest the 800, 888, 877 or 866 number. After you pick a toll-free phone number go to the checkout and pay for it.

COMPANY WEBSITE

Now you will need a company website; you can create this yourself or pay someone to do it for you. If you choose to do it yourself, I suggest that you use godaddy.com. But if you choose to pay someone to do it for you, download this app on your phone by the name of Fiverr. Once you download the Fiverr app, scroll through and find website creators.

Google search "godaddy.com", and once you are on the website you can start creating your website. This service should only cost you $30; prices do change daily but as of today the price is only $30.

Virtual Office and Address

Now we're at the point where you will be getting your corporate virtual office and virtual address. A virtual office uses a physical location that receives mail for you and will be an official business address for your company.

I- Postal 1

Google search "www.ipostal1.com". Once you are on the website you will be given several different packages to pick from. Choose the package that says "Virtual Business Address with Digital Mailbox". After you click the button to choose this package the website will send you to a different page with more options. When you are on this page choose "The Most Popular Package" which should be the "Green Package" and click on the sign-up button. After pressing the sign-up button on your green package, you will be sent to a different page which will be the "Choose Your Mailbox Location" page. Select your state and city, then you can pick your new business address. This service as of now should only cost you $9.99 per month. Go to the checkout page and pay for your new business office and address.

www.harborcompliance.com

Now it's time to buy a registered agent. A registered agent is someone whom you choose to receive official papers for your business. Paperwork like court papers, business registration renewal notices from the Secretary of State and tax notices from the IRS. When you file your LLC documents, you will be asked for your registered agent's information.

Google search "www.harborcompliance. com", and this company will act as your registered agent. Once you are on the website, click on the menu button, then go to the services section and find the registered agent button. After you fill out the information required, they will give you an address. This address will be used on your LLC filing documents. This service will only cost you $99.99 per year.

<u>Important Instructions</u>

There are three main reasons you need to get your business domain, email, phone number, virtual address, website and registered agent.

1. <u>Privacy </u>- You do not want to use any of your personal information when you file your LLC documents. If you do, your home address and other personal information will be a public record that anyone can see.

2. <u>Bank Loans</u> - When it's time to go to the bank and get the money bags for your business, they will look at all of these things first. If you do not have these things in place or they are personal addresses, phone numbers or emails, chances are high that they will not loan you any money. Why? Because you do not look like a real business!

3. <u>Separate Entity</u> The third reason you need all of these things is to separate yourself from your

business! You are not one with your business. You and your business are two separate entities!

LLC Documents S.O.S.

Now it's time to file your LLC paperwork. Google search "the Secretary of State" in your state first. Once you are on the website find the business filing section. Every state operates differently depending on the state that you are filing in. You may have to start an account with the S.O.S. to begin. Or you may have to go to the office to file. But in most states, you should be able to do it on the computer or print the papers out, fill them out and mail them to the office.

Once you have found out if you can file on the computer or mail the documents to complete the paperwork, you will use your new business email, 800 business number, virtual address and registered agent information to complete the process.

When they ask for the business's physical address and mailing address, put your virtual address for both of them.

There will be a section that asks for the member's name and address—member means owner of the company. Put your name as the member and the virtual office address as the member address.

The next section of questions depending on the order, will be the registered agent's information. Use your harbor compliance information to complete this section. Last but not least will be your business name. Use the business name that you reserved.

Now that your LLC documents are complete, mail them in or press send on the computer. Sit back and wait for a reply from the S.O.S. to see if your business is approved. Every state is different and the timeframe to receive your formation papers will be different. It could be immediately, or it may take a few days, but it won't be long.

Employer Identification Number (EIN)

An Employer Identification Number (EIN) is like your business's social security number. To receive your EIN you will need to go on to the IRS's website. IRS stands for Internal Revenue Service; these are the people that you pay taxes to. As you are applying for your EIN, you will be asked a lot of questions about your business for tax classification purposes. There are six primary ways a business can be classified for tax purposes: Sole proprietorship, partnership, C-Corporation, S-Corporation, LLC and non-profit.

3- Corporation Tax Classification

Even though you will be filing LLC paperwork, you do not want to pay taxes as a limited liability company.

You want the IRS to tax your company as an S-CORPORATION; this way you will pay less in taxes. Log on to www.irs.gov and find the section that says "File for EIN". Choose the Limited Liability Company (LLC) legal structure option. The next page will ask how many members there are; put one member if it's just you and your state. The next page will say that you will be classified as a disregarded entity. You do not want to accept the classification as a disregarded entity, therefore file Form 2553 S-Corporation status.

Dun & Bradstreet

Google search "Dun & Bradstreet". Once you are on the site find the section that says D-U-N-S number and apply for your business's number.

ASSETS AND LIABILITIES

ASSET

An asset is a resource with economic (money) value that a person or business owns or controls that will provide monetary benefits now or in the future.

In other words, an asset is anything that you spend your money on that will put money in your pocket now or in the future. Items that you can sell for a higher price than what you paid for them. Products that hold value and appreciate over time. Appreciate means that the value of the item will increase in the future. Let's say you buy a house today for $50,000 and ten years later the value rises to $80,000.

Some examples of assets would be owning a profitable business, franchise ownership, dump trucks, 18-wheelers, stocks and bonds, rental property, farmland, cash money, good credit, gold bars, gold coins, crude oil, whole life insurance policy, royalties, intellectual property, copyrights, art and standard Rolex watches. Those are some but not all of the different types of assets in this world. Your time is your most valuable asset!

Once you spend it, you can never ever get it back. Material and physical assets can be lost and gotten again but time is gone for good once it's gone. Therefore, spend as much time as you can per day on income producing activities.

Assets put money in your pocket, add to your net worth and increase your value.

Before you buy anything, ask yourself: "Will this make me some money? How can this increase my net worth?"

Liability

A liability is defined as a debt that is owed by a person or business. In other words, a liability is anything that takes money out of your pocket—products and services that you spend money on that will not bring money back to you. Products that you buy which lose value. For example, the dream car you want that may cost $100,000; after you buy it, the value of it goes down (depreciate), and in a few years it will only be worth $50,000. Those Michael Jordan shoes you love, after you wear them for a while, you will not be able to sell them for the same price you paid for them because the value has depreciated.

The house you live in is a liability because you pay rent or mortgage monthly and it takes money out of your pocket consistently.

Examples of Liabilities

Some examples of liabilities are clothes, shoes, food, phone bill, cable bill, internet bill, car maintenance, gas bill, water bill, car insurance, renter's insurance, furniture, kids, daycare, student loans and also some people. Yes, people can be a liability.

Turn Liabilities into Assets

Find ways to turn your liabilities into assets. On a small scale, charge your friends money to borrow your toys, get money from friends to let them ride on your bike, 4-wheeler, go-kart or motorcycle, if you have any of those. If you like to eat candy and snacks, buy a lot of it so you can sell some. That way it would be as if you are eating your portion of the snacks for free. Don't give all of your old clothes and shoes to a thrift store but sell them yourself. On a larger scale, when you get a car, rent it out on Turo and other platforms. When you get a house, rent out the rooms; this is called "house hacking". Turn the bills that you pay into a credit history by using the credit building knowledge I gave you in chapter one.

ASSETS	LIABILITIES
1 kilo of gold	Mercedes-Benz car
Dump truck	Toyota Camry car
Rolex watch	Gucci purse
4-plex (multifamily)	The house you live in
18-wheeler	Fendi clothes
Buying a franchise	Student loans
Buying shares of Apple	iPhone
Land	Motorcycle

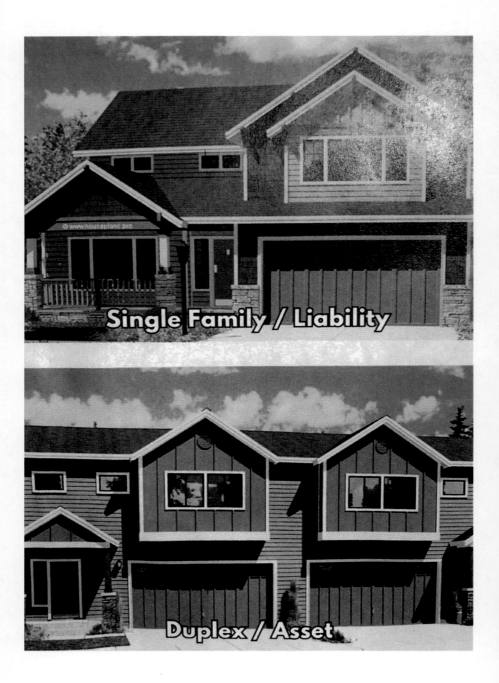

Single Family / Liability

Duplex / Asset

Triplex / Asset

Four plex / Asset

REAL ESTATE

WHAT IS REAL ESTATE?

Real estate is a form of real property, meaning that it is something you own that is attached to a piece of land. It can be used for residential, commercial or industrial purposes.

Real estate is first, the ground that you walk on and drive on, all the land you see with trees on it. Real estate is all of the buildings you see attached to the ground except mobile homes, shopping malls, houses, apartments, schools, libraries, hospitals, fast food restaurants, gas stations, night clubs, prisons, hotels, motels, storage facilities, car lots, grocery stores, clothing stores, daycares, barber shops, beauty salons, churches, gyms, warehouses, truck stops, farmland, and more. These are all businesses but they needed real estate to start and run the business.

Real estate is an asset, an asset that can last for generations. 90% of all millionaires became millionaires by real estate investing.

You can become a real estate investor and own real estate with bad credit, but it will be more challenging than it otherwise would be. To make your journey easy, build a good credit score and credit history. I will show you multiple ways to gain ownership of real estate.

Federal Housing Administration (FHA) Loan

The FHA loan program is a government insured mortgage loan. It was created by the federal government for first time home buyers. You will need a credit score of 580 and good credit history, proof of income, and no previous homeownership in the past 3 years from the date you apply. The home must be your primary residence for 12 months (you must live in the house 12 months). The down payment is only 3.5% of the price of the house. If the house is $100,000 you will only pay a down payment of $3,500 which is 3.5% of $100,000.

USDA Loan Program

The USDA loan program is a loan program backed by the U.S. Department of Agriculture as part of its Rural Development Guaranteed Housing Loan program. With this program you do not have to pay a down payment. The home must be in an eligible rural area, which the USDA defines as a population of less than 20,000 people. You must live in the home, and it must be your primary residence. You must have a stable income and a credit score of 640 or higher.

NACA PROGRAM

The NACA Program is a non-profit organization started in 1988. NACA stands for Neighborhood Assistance Corporation of America. With this program, you do not pay anything upfront. No down payment, no closing cost, no fees and no credit check. They will ask for bank statements, tax returns and they will ask a lot of questions about your monthly expenses. The main requirements of this program are to have steady income and several months of the monthly mortgage payments saved in your bank account. You have the option to build a single-family home or multifamily property brand new or buy one that is for sale on the market. This would be a great way to get your first 4-plex property.

When you sign up, they will put you through a 3-hour workshop and explain every little detail about the program to you.

NACA

QUALIFICATION WORKBOOK

BECOME A HOMEOWNER

THROUGH ▸ NACA'S COMPREHENSIVE COUNSELING
WITH ▸ NACA'S BEST IN AMERICA MORTGAGE

MEMBER'S NAME: _____

DATE OF WORKSHOP: _____

NACA ID #: _____

WWW.NACA.COM

Fighting Financial Exploitation with America's Best Mortgage

NACA MORTGAGE

No Down Payment

No Closing Costs

No Mortgage Insurance

No Consideration of Credit Score

No Perfect Credit Required

Interest Rate Below Market

Stabilizing Neighborhoods through ADVOCACY and ACTIVIST MEMBERS

BUY A 4-UNIT PROPERTY

Using the FHA and NACA program is a good way to get your first property. Lenders/banks categorize 1-4-unit properties under the single-family property umbrella. That means that a house and a 4-Plex is the same to them. 5 units and above is considered to be commercial real estate. The goal is for your first property to be a duplex (2-unit), tri-plex (3-units) or 4-plex (4-unit) property. Live in one and rent out the other ones. You will get the big mansion later on in life; right now income producing assets are the focus.

Why does Your 1st Property Need to be Multifamily?

Your first property needs to be multifamily, specifically a 4-unit because this is a money producing asset that will put money in your pocket and you will have people living in the other units paying the mortgage bill for you. You can live in one of the units free depending on cost of the mortgage bill and how much you charge for rent on the other units.

Do not purchase a 1-unit single family home for your first place to live in. You will be obligated to pay that mortgage bill yourself for 15-30 years. If you miss a few payments the bank will foreclose (take your house) on your house. 15-30 years is a long-term commitment to pay for something, therefore you want someone else to pay that bill for you. Any properties you own you want to rent it out and let someone else pay the mortgage, not you!

After the tenant (the person you rent it to) builds enough equity by paying the mortgage you can go to the bank and borrow that money to buy more properties.

If you live in it and have been paying the mortgage, then pull out the equity; you will only be pulling out your own money that you have already paid. Play the game, don't let the game play you.

Investor/ Entrepreneur Side of the Table

In this section, you will be looking at real estate from the eyes of an investor/entrepreneur. You will learn about different investor real estate loans, how to find distressed and discounted properties, buying real estate through the stock market, and non-traditional ways to acquire property.

Distressed Properties and Motivated Sellers

When you hear the phrase distressed properties that simply means raggedy properties that need to be fixed up. The term "motivated seller" means that a person is eager to sell their property because they are in a bad situation and need quick cash. Being motivated could also mean that they have inherited property from a relative that has passed away and they just do not want it. The name of the game is finding deeply discounted deals when you are not building brand new properties from the ground up. Targeting distressed properties and motivated sellers is how most investors find deals.

How to Find Distressed Properties

You can find raggedy run-down real estate by simply getting in a car and just taking a ride. Another way to find distressed property is to go to your city's public information section on their website and find the "Public records" category. The public records that you are requesting are "Code Violations". The city pays people to ride around neighborhoods to find damaged properties, abandoned properties and properties with high grass. Once they find the property, they put a note on the door stating that the property is in violation of city rules. After they mark the property for violations the property is put on the code violations list and recorded in the public records department of the city.

If you have trouble finding the code violations list on the website, call the city and ask them to direct you to the department that holds the "Property Code Violations" records. When you find the department tell them you want all of the properties that have been marked for "high grass, damaged structure and abandoned" for the last 60 days.

Skip Tracing

Skip tracing is the process of finding the owners of the distressed properties that investors want to buy. This is a very important part of the process that can make or break your success. If you can't find the owner, you can't buy the property.

Tax Assessor Office

When you find a property you want to buy, the first thing you do is Google search the tax assessor's website, then type in the address of the property and it will tell you who has been paying the taxes which is most likely to be the owner of the property. The owner will most likely be a person, a business or a trust fund.

If the property is owned by a business, you will have to Google search the name of the business and find out who the owner is. Once you get the name of the owner it is now time to get to work.

Free Skip Tracing

Once you have the name of the possible owner, Google search "www.fastpeoplesearch.com" and "www.truepeoplesearch .com". These are two free ways of finding the phone numbers, e-mails and addresses of these property owners. Once you have a list of numbers, emails and addresses, use all of them or at least the first 3 on each list.

Paid Skip Tracing

PropStream, BatchLeads, Fiverr, Batch Skip Tracing, Lead Sherpa, Versium search, and

DealMachine: all of these will help you find the owners of the properties you want to buy quickly, but you will have to pay. Some will require you to sign up with them and pay a monthly membership fee anywhere from $49 to $100 per month. Some will only charge you for the properties that you want to look up.

Motivated Sellers

Motivated sellers are people that may be eager to sell their property for far less than the value. Therefore, you have the chance of getting a $200,000 property for $125,000. Now that's a good deal.

Most investors get lists from the courthouse to find these motivated sellers. Probate (people who have died and left property to relatives), pre-foreclosure (people about to lose their house), foreclosure, and tax delinquent (people who have not paid property taxes to the government).To get these lists, call your local courthouse and ask someone how you can get these public records. You may have to go to the court or maybe you can get them from their website. But, call to get the correct answer because every city and state does not operate the same.

Owner Finance Properties

With this strategy you do not need to show any of your bank statements, credit score and history, or W-2's but you will need a down payment.

Owner financing means that the owner of the property will act as the bank and cut the bank out of the deal. Therefore, you will be making a one-on-one deal, just you and the owner. These types of deals are done with properties that are "free and clear". Free and clear means that the owner does not owe anything on the property, it is paid off in full.

Websites like Zillow and Redfin have a section called "FSBO": For Sale by Owner. What you would do is call this property and simply ask the owner if they are willing to do an "Owner Finance Deal". If they do not know what it is, tell them you will give them a down payment and pay them monthly until the property is paid in full.

Example of Owner Finance Deal

1. Cost of property: $100,000 Down Payment: $5,000 Monthly payment: $300 30 years (360 months): $108,000

   A. Multiply monthly payment price ($300) times the months (360 months). This will give you the amount you will be paying over 30 years, which is 360 months. The amount is $108,000.

   B. Add the down payment and $108,000, which will give you the offer price of $113,000.The owner has the property for sale at $100,000, so offer him $113,000.

$13,000 will be the interest fee for him or her financing the deal.

Before you call a property owner about buying their property through owner financing, do the calculations like the one in the example to make them an offer price.

You determine the offer price, the down payment price, the monthly payment price, and how long it will take you to pay off the property. The terms can be 5 years, 6 years, 10 years, 12 years or 20 years—it's all your decision, and the owner can simply say yes or no. If the owner says no, give them a few different offers.

Subject-To

Subject-To is short for subject to the existing mortgage. These types of deals are properties where people still owe money to the bank and have a mortgage on them. With this strategy you will simply be taking over the payments. Your name will go on the deed of the property but not on the mortgage.

Investor Real Estate Loans

In this section, I will tell you about the types of loans that real estate entrepreneurs use to acquire property. Before we get to those loans, I want you to understand why real estate investors use loans. First off, lenders have way more money than investors do. An entrepreneur will run out of money before the banks and lenders will. Let's look at the game from a large scale first. Let's say you have $1 billion in the bank. The high-rise hotel you want to build will cost you $1 billion. After you have invested the billion dollars in the hotel project, you don't have any money to do other projects. Now, how long will it take you to make enough money for another super big project?

Now let's look at the game from a smaller point of view. Let's say you have $500,000 in the bank and you want to build a 4-plex that will cost $500,000 to build. Once again, after you find this project, you don't have any more money for another project at this time.

Use your money to pay for the down payment of the property and let the lender be your partner on the project to pay the larger portion of the cost of the project. You will need good credit to use these loans, and every lender will have different requirements.

HARD MONEY LOANS

This type of loan is used to buy discounted and distressed properties. They are short-term loans usually from 6 months to 24 months or longer depending on the lender. Hard money loans are short-term because they are used for you to buy the property, fix the property, sell the property for profit then pay the lender back.

You can find hard money lenders by Google searching "hard money lenders". Some hard money lenders give loans to investors in all 50 states, some loan in a few states and some only loan to people in the state that their company office is located.

DSCR Loan

DSCR stands for Debt Service Coverage Ratio. With this type of loan it is all about how much money the property will make monthly. Will the property make enough money to pay you and pay the loan back. You will need a good credit score and a down payment, but you will not have to show any job income information such as tax returns, check stubs, or bank statements.

The DSCR Loan is used to buy commercial apartment buildings up to 10 units. With this type of loan there is no limit to how many loans you can get at one time. To find DSCR Lenders just go to your faithful information friend Google, and he will show you all of the DSCR lenders.

HELOC

HELOC stands for Home Equity Line of Credit and it is a secured loan. With the HELOC loan your property will be used as collateral.

Therefore, if you do not pay the loan back, the lender keeps your property.

To qualify for a HELOC you will need to have enough equity in your property. Also, the lender will look at your credit score, credit history, employment history, monthly income and monthly debt.

PRIVATE LENDERS

Private money/private lenders are people or organizations that lend money and are not tied to any major banks or corporations. Four types of private lenders are: private individuals, a private equity fund or private equity firm, a family office and a hedge fund.

Private loans can be approved and funded in a few hours or a few days at the latest. They also require less personal financial information from you.

The lenders are less concerned about your income, credit score or your real estate investing history.

How to Find Private Lenders

1. Google search "private money lenders" in your city and state.

2. Join private money lender groups on Facebook.

3. Google search "www.realestatewealthnetwork.com" and once you are on the website, click the button that says "private lenders".

You will have to pay for this information, but it is well worth it. As of today, the cost is $300 per year.

The Private Lender Data Feed is the name of the service, and it will show you every private lender in the United States of America!

Real Estate Wealth Network.com
8805 Route 415, Cambell, NY 14821-9703
Phone: (607) 527-6097
Email: info@rewn.com

Non-QM Loans

Non-QM is short for Non-Qualifying Mortgage loan. These loans were designed for entrepreneurs and self-employed individuals that do not have check stubs and W-2's. These lenders use your bank statements to qualify you for a loan. The lender will look at all of your deposits from the past 12-24 months, depending on the lender. The down payment will be higher than a conventional loan, usually 20% of the purchase price or greater.

R.E.I.T.

R.E.I.T. stands for Real Estate Investment Trust. This way of real estate investing is done through the stock market. The great part about R.E.I.T. stock is that they will pay you monthly or quarterly (every three months).

A lot of the stores you shop at do not own the building that they are doing business at. They rent the building from real estate companies. Therefore, you can own the company that owns the building, and when the real estate company receives rent payments, they will pay you.

Agree Realty Corporation (ADC)

Agree Realty Corporation (ADC) is a company that owns and rents buildings to the following businesses:

- Walmart
- Tractor Supply Co.
- Dollar General
- Best Buy
- TJX Cos. Inc.
- O'Reilly
- CVS Pharmacy
- Dollar Tree
- Hobby Lobby
- Kroger
- Lowe's
- Sherwin-Williams
- Burlington
- Home Depot
- AutoZone
- LA Fitness

As of today, one share of Agree Realty is $66.84.

Realty Income Corp (O)

Realty Income Corp owns and rents buildings to the following businesses:

- Dollar General
- Walgreens
- 7-Eleven
- Dollar Tree
- Wynn Resorts
- Fed Ex
- LA Fitness
- Red Lobster
- Regal Cinemas
- Home Depot
- Kroger
- Tesco
- Sainsbury's
- B+Q
- CVS Pharmacy
- Lifetime Fitness
- Walmart/Sam's Club

- AMC Theaters
- Tractor Supply

As of today, one share of Realty Income Corp is $61.07.

Kimco Realty

Kimco Realty owns and rents buildings to:

- TJX Cos. Inc.
- Home Depot
- Albertsons
- Ross
- Walmart
- Hobby Lobby
- Whole Food
- Pet Smart
- Kroger
- Burlington
- Ahold Delhaize
- Marshalls
- Bed Bath + Beyond

- Target
- Dick's Sporting Goods

As of today, one share of Kimco is $19.10.

MARKETING

Marketing is promoting and advertising your products or services, trying to get people to buy them. First, you are letting people know that your product or service is available for them to buy. If people don't know about your product or service, they can't buy them from you. Secondly, you may offer deals, discounts and bargains to influence them to buy from you.

YOU SEE MARKETING EVERYWHERE

When you turn on the TV, logon to Facebook, Instagram, TikTok or Twitter you see people and businesses trying to get you to buy something! This is marketing! Have you ever seen the commercial featuring Shaq—the retired professional basketball player—trying to sell you insurance? That is marketing. Have you ever seen the commercial of Lil Wayne the rapper pouring champagne on the smart phone? That too is marketing! What about when you are riding in the car and see signs on the light poles and stop signs that might say, "Garage sale," or "Lawn Service $40" or "We buy houses".

All of those are marketing tactics, and you can use them to sell your products and services too.

A.B.M.

A.B.M. stands for "Always Be Marketing". Marketing is an all day, every day thing you need to do to bring sales to your business. No matter how much success you have or how well your business is doing, you still should be marketing!

Think about the big companies worth billions and trillions of dollars, you still see them on TV and social media telling you about a new product they have for sale or about a big discount sale they are having.

The beauty of owning your own business and being your own boss is that there is no limit to how much money you can make!! Every place you go and every person you meet should know about your business; keep business cards and flyers close to you whenever you leave home. Pass them out to everybody you come in contact with. Get yourself some shirts made with your company name and phone numbers on them, and wear them daily! You wear all the name brand companies' clothes like Nike, Reebok, Puma, and Jordan—you walk around and advertise for them every day! Wear your own company clothes and advertise for yourself!

You want to hit them from every angle consistently and persistently! Be in their minds when they wake up, be in their thoughts all through the day and make them dream about your company when they go to sleep.

You want to tattoo your company's products and services on their brain visually (seeing) and auditorily (hearing) by using both the old ways of marketing and the new ways of marketing.

TRADITIONAL MARKETING

Traditional Marketing means the old ways of marketing before the internet was popular. The old ways are still effective but some of them will require a little leg work.

<u>Traditional Ways of Marketing</u>

- TVRadio
- Newspaper
- Car magnet
- Yard sign
- Billboard
- Tee-shirts
- Pop-up shops
- Business cards
- Word of mouth

- Flyer

TV, Radio, Billboards and Newspapers

These ways of marketing are still used today, and they work. Google search the local TV station, radio, newspaper and billboards in your city to find the phone numbers and contact information of these businesses, then ask them for pricing and information about their advertising services.

Fast Signs

Fast Signs is the name of a marketing company that makes car magnets, yard signs, business cards, flyers, and banners. They are very popular in many different cities. I would suggest that you Google search multiple different companies and compare pricing to get the best deal. You may have to get a designer to design a company flyer and car magnets before you can get them created. Just call around and ask questions; they will tell you what you need to do to get them created.

- **Car Magnets:** On your car magnets put your company name, business number, email and social media contact info.
- **Yard Signs:** On your yard signs do not put your company name! All you need on your yard signs is a phone number and the product or service you are offering. Keep it short and straight to the point! We Cut Trees 1-800-444-0000"/ "Mobile Car Wash 1-800-111-0130"/"Tutoring Classes 1-877-430-1988"/"We Paint Houses 1-866-322-4481"/ "Cheap Floor Installation 1-800-266-1530"/"School Clothes for Sale 1-800-134-4111".

You may get a call from the city telling you to take them down. This is not a criminal offense, and you cannot and will not be arrested but someone might call you and ask you to remove the signs in certain places. Do not be afraid, business is a risk and life is a risk every day! I can promise you if there is a demand and desire for the products or services you are selling, these signs will get your phone ringing almost instantly!

Flyers:

Create your flyers exactly like your car magnets. They should match the magnets, and you only need the words on one side.

Banners:

Banners are like small portable billboards. They are made in different sizes. The biggest may be 8 feet by 10 feet depending on the company that makes them. Make these just like your car magnets and flyers.

Putting Out Yard Signs

There are companies that you can pay to place your signs, but I would suggest that you do this yourself. Sign placement companies have been known to take your money and not put up your signs.

Where to Put the Signs

The idea of the signs is to put them where lots of people will see them. These places and locations are called high traffic areas. You will put them on light poles, traffic lights, stop signs and traffic signs. Put them on the light poles and stop signs at businesses like Home Depot, Lowe's, Walmart, Sam's Club, Target, shopping malls, barber shops, beauty salons, outlets, churches and grocery stores. All of these places are high traffic areas.

Find the most popular and busy streets in your city that has a lot of traffic and place the signs on the poles of the red lights. This type of street should have 4-way traffic with red lights on each corner in each direction. Put them on the poles. Simply park on the side of the road, put the emergency flashers on and walk to each pole. You can do this on the weekends or times of the day when traffic is low.

Apartment Complexes and Neighborhoods

Place them on the stop signs in apartment complexes and neighborhoods. You only need to place them at the entrance and exit points where residents come in and leave. Some neighborhoods have "no solicitation" signs posted; if you see these signs do not put up any flyers or signs.

How to Hang the Signs

Go to Home Depot, Lowe's or Walmart and buy Zip Ties, the longest ones you can find in the store. Poke two holes in the middle of your yard signs about 3-4 inches apart. Insert the zip tie in one of the holes from the side of the sign that does not have words on it.

Run the zip tie through the front side, bend it then insert it in the other hole to make it come out the back where the connector part of the zip tie is. Put the sign on the pole with the words showing and connect the zip tie. For the big light poles you will need 2-4 zip ties to fit around the pole, and for the stop signs you will only need one.

Business Cards

On the business cards put your name, business number, email, and company information. Fast Signs can make these for you as well, but I would suggest that you Google search "business card creators" and find the cheapest deal. Keep these in your pocket at all times. Remember the motto. A.B.M.- Always be marketing.

Tee-Shirts

If you do not know anyone personally that makes tee-shirts, ask around or simply do a Google search on the internet. On these shirts you only need your company name and business number. Start off with just a few for you to wear. Later on get shirts made for your family and friends to wear and remind them every so often to wear them in public. They will become walking billboards for your business. When you make enough money to get lots of them made, do that and sell them.

Pop-Up Shops

Pop-Up shops are events where people set up booths and tables to sell their products, like an outside flea market, so to speak. But there is one in particular I want to tell you about that is specifically for kids. The name of it is ACTON Children's Business Fair. Google search the company and sign up to attend the event and sell your products!

Every Door Direct Mail (EDDM)

Every Door Direct Mail (EDDM) is a service provided by the US Postal Service where they will put your flyers in every mailbox in your city. This will cost money, but it is an easy way to get your flyers in the hands of potential customers. Google search "the US Postal Service". When you are on the website, find the EDDM section. They will walk you through the steps to get those flyers into the mailboxes of houses and other businesses.

Passing Out Flyers by Hand

For this way of putting out flyers, hire the homeless people. Give them clean used clothes to put on, put them in back of a truck and take them to the high traffic parking lots like Walmart and put the flyers on the cars. You should only need about 5-6 people and give them about $20-$40 apiece and feed them; they will be grateful. Do this about once a month but make sure to get all of the big parking lots.

Start off small with five shirts for you to wear daily. Get 200 yard signs and put out 50 signs per week. Get 1,000 flyers made and 500 business cards.

Dream Clients

Dream Clients are people or businesses that you think would spend a lot of money on your products or services for a long time, maybe even a lifetime.

Let's say you designed and created specially made socks that basketball players love to wear. The NBA players would be your target Dream Clients. They have lots of money, they love basketball socks and if you could get them to buy your socks, they would probably buy socks from you for the rest of their life.

Marketing to Dream Clients

There are about 450 NBA players in the league. What you would do is focus on marketing to 30 of them to start with. You want to flood them with your advertising and promotion! Do research on them, get as much personal contact information as you can on them. That information should consist of emails, addresses, social media accounts, phone numbers, and any other way you think you could get your message and product in their mind.

How Often to Contact Dream Clients

Email

- If you were to get their email address, send them emails every day! 2-3 times a day on some days.

Home address

- Mail them flyers two times a week and send them one pair of free socks one time only. Put two yard signs near the entrance and exit points of their neighborhood. Somewhere they will see it when they leave home and somewhere they will see it when they return home.

Phone numbers

- If you were to get their phone number, send a picture of your company flyer to their text message one time per month.

Social media account

- If you find them on social media, send your company flyer to their DM (direct message) twice a week, or more.

The object of marketing is to constantly be seen and heard by your target audience, to the point where they say to themselves, "Let me buy something so they can leave me alone" or "Let me hear what they are talking about". The squeaky wheel gets the oil!

Cold Calling

I didn't put this old method of marketing in the list of traditional marketing methods, but this is a strategy that is still used today; it is effective, but time consuming and can be a headache. Cold calling is calling people and businesses that do not know you and you have never talked to them before in your life. You know those unwanted calls you get from strangers trying to sell you something? Yes, that is what you call cold calling.

"Hi Mrs. Mary, my name is_____ calling from_____I was just trying to see if you were interested in having your house pressure washed any time soon?" This is an example of a cold calling script. To be honest with you, you will be hung up on, cursed out and ignored but this strategy is still used daily by businesses.

The New Ways of Marketing

Of course, you already know all of the new ways of marketing that are done on the internet. Google, Twitter, YouTube, Instagram, email, Facebook, TikTok, Netflix and Tubi are the most common platforms where internet marketing and advertising is done.

On these platforms you will need to open professional business accounts in order to create and pay for ads. The word ads is short for advertisement and with ads you will be creating short commercials to be shown on the social media platforms.

You will also need to reach out to people that have a lot of followers and ask them to advertise your business on their pages. There are a lot of people doing this now, and they will charge you money, but it will be worth it.

You will also need to join Facebook groups. In the Facebook groups that you choose you want to network with people and advertise your products.

Test and Measure

The phrase "Test and Measure" means that you are tracking and monitoring your marketing strategies to see which ones are working and which ones are not working.

How to Test and Measure

Testing and measuring is easy. You ask every person that contacts you about buying something from you, "How did you hear about my company ?" and they will tell you without any difficulty.

Once you find out, keep a record of it. This is very, very, very, very important; you need to know and must know what marketing strategies are not working so you can stop doing them and focus more attention and money on the ones that are working!

With each marketing strategy—the old ones and the new ones—you want to start small, just do a little bit of each one, then sit back and wait for a reply from the customers. When the calls and messages start coming in, you began asking each and every one of them, "How did you hear about the company?"

Marketing is the heartbeat of any and every business. No matter how great your product or service is, if people don't know about it, they cannot buy from you! And no matter how big your business is, if the sales stop, the business stops. Marketing and advertising is what brings the sales that bring the mail (money)!

A.B.M. - Always

Be Marketing!!

BUILDING A TEAM

When I speak of a team, I mean recruiting all of the people you will need to help you on your journey of wealth, power and riches. You need a team because you cannot do everything yourself and you can't build wealth alone. In the beginning of your entrepreneur journey you may have to wear many hats (do a lot of different jobs and tasks) within your business. Having a team will make your life as an entrepreneur/investor a lot easier.

WHO DO YOU NEED ON YOUR TEAM?

The first and probably the most important type of people you need on your team is people with experience, knowledge, wisdom and information about the businesses that you choose to indulge in. Coaches, mentors, advisors and tour guides. People who have done what you are attempting to do, people who have been where you are headed.

These people can give you information on what to do and what not to do. It's like having a tour guide through a place you have never been before.

You can learn from their mistakes and losses, so you will not have to take the same losses and will not have to make the same mistakes. You have to find these people by any means necessary! Have you ever heard of the saying "The game is to be sold, not told?" Most people live by this saying, therefore do not expect these people to give you knowledge for free—you will be setting yourself up for disappointment! If you have to pay for the game (knowledge/information), pay for it! Nothing in life is free so don't expect it. If you cannot get face-to-face with the person or people, you need to see if they have written a book and buy it.

Success leaves a trail, and you need to be on that trail. For any and every business you choose, somebody has most likely done it already and many have written about it. But first try to create a face-to-face relationship with them.

The Type of Players You Need

The business you choose will decide exactly the type of players you will need on your team. Any business you choose you will need lawyers to do contracts, CPAs for tax knowledge and services, qualified/certified workers and maybe laborers. You want the best players money can buy. Sometimes when you go the cheap route it will cost you double, because you have to go back and correct mistakes.

Screen Them Before You Sign Them

This is very, very important and prevents you from wasting time and money! Before you put them on your team you need to know for sure that they can do a great job at what they say they can do. Find and ask people who they have done business with, people who they have done work for about their work performance. Read internet reviews about them, or their business. Ask the person you are hiring a lot of questions, give them a small task to do, a test. Make them show and prove to you in some kind of way that they are good at what they do. People will lie, lie ,lie and lie some more for a job opportunity! Screen them before you put them on your team!

Example of Team Building

Take me for an example in writing this book. I have read a lot of books in my life, but I have never written one. Yes, this is the first but not the last book I will write. These are all of the people I needed on my team to make this happen:

- Typist
- Book Editor
- Book Format Guy
- Book Cover Designer
- ISBN/Barcode Provider

- Mentor
- Publisher

How to Find Your Team Players

Finding the people you need is easy—use Google search to find professionals like lawyers and CPAs and also ask around for recommendations. Create a business account on Indeed.com and post job offerings for the type of workers/employees you need to hire. Join job groups on Facebook and post job offerings. Download this app on your phone by the name of "Fiverr"! Go to the local unemployment office and register your business with them. Depending on your city, the unemployment office will allow you to hold job fairs at the office or put your company on the list to hold job fairs at different locations.

Keeping Your Word

Keeping your word with your team is more valuable than money. People believing that you will do what you told them you will do is like having good credit. Do not sell them dreams, since this will destroy the trust and confidence they have in you.

Think three times before you make a commitment or make a promise. If you tell them you are going to do something, do it! Life happens and sometimes situations come upon you and prevent you from keeping your word, which is understandable. Other than that, keep your word.

Feed Your Team Well

You see how the big companies that have trillions and billions of dollars pay their workers pennies ? No, not you, you are different! Therefore, you will operate differently! Don't be greedy, make sure everybody eats as good as you do. Give them bonuses, give them extra money if they are an asset to your team. Without a team you are nothing. Just imagine if all of Amazon or

Walmart workers quit, I mean every last one of them! How would they keep the business going? They probably couldn't. Take care of your team, and your team will take care of you! Feed your team and your team will feed you!

PROTECT YOUR RICHES

It's not about getting money; it's about keeping the money! You must get the money, grow the money and keep the money!

Pass it on to the next generation; your kids, grandkids, great-grandkids, great-great-grandkids and your whole bloodline. Making the money live forever is the goal. Rich forever! You have to protect your assets from any and everything that can take it away from you. The first thing that could cause your family wealth to disappear is the ignorance of not knowing how to protect the paper (money). Therefore, the first step to protecting your riches is educating yourself on how to protect it! There are a lot of different ways and tactics the rich use to protect their wealth. I will tell you about some of those in this chapter.

TRUST FUNDS

Trust funds are legal entities that provide financial (money), tax and legal protection for people. Trust funds can hold a variety of assets such as money, real estate property, stocks, bonds, a business and any other assets that an individual or business may own.

Asset Protection Trust

An asset protection trust is often used to protect a person's assets from creditors (businesses you may owe money to), lawsuits (people who may try to take you to court, sue you and take your money) and any judgements against your assets.

Totten Trust Fund

This particular asset protection trust is used for your money in a bank account. The money in the bank account will avoid probate court and go directly to the people you choose to leave it to.

It is only to be used for money. It is also called a (POD)—Payable on Death.

Offshore Trust Funds

This type of trust fund is set up in a different country outside of the United States. Some say that this is the best form of protection from creditors, even though real estate property is not protected in this type of trust fund. The list below will give you the best places to open an offshore trust fund:

- Belize
- Cook Islands
- Nevis
- Luxembourg
- Cayman Islands
- British Virgin Islands

Dynasty Trust

The dynasty trust is a lifetime long-term trust created to pass wealth from generation to generation without being taxed, as long as the asset remains in the trust. The assets in the trust pass down to the children first. After all the children have passed away the assets go to the grandchildren. If the assets stay inside the trust, divorce cannot take the assets from the children or grandchildren. Therefore, someone cannot marry into the family, divorce your children or grandchildren and take any assets!

Living Trust

A living trust is a private document, so the public cannot see the value of your assets nor can the public see the assets that are listed in the trust fund. This type of trust adds privacy to your legacy. It is called a Living Trust because they are created now while you are living. In this trust you can put:

- Bank Accounts
- Real Estate Property
- Whole Life Insurance Policies
- Stocks, Bonds & Investment Assets

- Tangible personal property like vehicles, antiques, silver, gold, artwork, collectibles, furniture, machinery and equipment
- Intellectual property such as patents, trademarks, copyrights and trade secrets.
- LLC's, limited liability companies
- Cryptocurrency

Trustee Grantor Beneficiary

It takes three parties to create a trust. A grantor is the person that creates the trust and puts assets into the trust. A trustee is like a middleman that manages the trust fund to make sure that the rules of the trust are followed; this person should be a third-party person like a lawyer. The beneficiaries are the people who will receive the assets and benefits, people from the trust like kids and grandkids for example.

Patents ,Trademarks and Copyrights

Protect your intellectual property by using patents, trademarks and copyrights. A patent protects new inventions, processes or scientific creations, a trademark protects brands, logos and slogans and a copyright protects original works of authorship. For example, this book has been copyrighted and will last 70 years after I'm dead. Therefore, when I'm gone to glory, my kids and grandkids will receive money from the sales of this book. My Logo "Black Billionaire 1.25" is a brand, slogan and logo all in one and is protected by a trademark.

Pre-Nuptial Agreements

A pre-nuptial agreement is a contract between two people who plan on getting married. The contract is made before the man and woman get married. A pre-nup is a plan of what will happen to the assets if the two divorce. It is designed to protect what you have before the marriage. I know you will have a lot of assets before you get married, therefore, I know you will file a pre-nuptial agreement before you get married, right!

Lawyers

There are a lot of different types of trust funds as I have shown you. You should hire a lawyer for your trust fund needs and your pre-nup agreement as well. A good estate planning lawyer knows or should know exactly which types of trust funds you will need for the different assets you need to protect and hide. The lawyer will also create these documents for you.

YOU ARE AN ASSET, PROTECT YOURSELF

Protect your heart, mind, spirit and body. Protect your heart from those that don't deserve your love (do not give your pearls to swine), protect your mind from negativity, doubts, stress, worry, ignorance, fear and deception. Protect your spirit from bad spirits and bad energy of others. Protect your body from physical violent harm (don't let anybody hurt you) and the self-destruction that bad eating habits bring. Stay away from dairy products (milk, eggs, cheese), meat (steak, chicken and pork), fish and processed foods!

Gun violence in the world is at an all-time high and the innocent die daily from gun violence. Use your mind to avoid places where violence occurs often. Secondly, always be prepared to prevent and defend yourself against deadly bodily injury according to the law. Educate yourself on state and federal self-defense laws, castle doctrine and stand your ground laws. Use your 2nd Amendment rights—the right to bear arms.

Websites like www.bulletproofzone.com sell all kinds of bulletproof items like bulletproof tank top tee-shirts, bulletproof hoodies, bulletproof coats, and bulletproof backpacks and vests.

www.armormax.com is a website where you can buy bulletproof cars. The president rides in a bulletproof car and you should to. You are just as important as the president. Protect the brand!

* Show me your friends and I'll show you your future

The phrase "Show me your friends and I'll Show you your future" means that you will become like the people you hang around! When I say hang around, I mean the people you listen to, take advice from, the people you spend time with, the people you talk to and the people you trust. If you spend time with and hang around 9 millionaires chances are that you will become the 10th millionaire in the group. This saying is very true and a fact of life and applies to any and everyone you come in contact with. Everybody should not be a part of your day to day life even family members.

You have to practice social distancing just as people were forced to do during the outbreak of the 2020 Covid-19 sickness. You can love, and help people from a distance, I like to call it feeding them with a fishing pole just like you do when you fish, keeping your distance so their ways and thoughts do not rub off on you. Attitudes are contagious. In the beginning of time when God created humans God created Adam and Eve. A man and a woman to be together. No matter what you see on television, the internet or when you are in public. Two men or two women were not meant or made to be lovers or married to one another. If God made you an a woman be that. If God made you a man be that! Dress like a women if you are a woman, Dress like a man if you were born to be a man. Be in this world not of this world! Separate yourself, come from among them. I Love you and God loves you, protect yourself.

WHOLE LIFE INSURANCE POLICY

The Whole Life Insurance Policy is the type of insurance policy you need; do not get a life insurance policy with terms of 10, 20, or 30 years! A whole life insurance policy is a life insurance policy where you can borrow the money that you have put in it and the beneficiaries will still be paid when you die. This is another way to save and hide your family money, then pass it on to the next generation.

It is very, very, very important that when you sit down with the life insurance agent (the person that sells life insurance and does the paperwork) that your power to borrow money from your policy is written in the contract. Do not sign the paperwork if it is not written in the agreement. Another tip is to get the contract from the agent and take it to a lawyer before signing it.

There are two sides to a Whole Life Insurance Policy—"a life side" to borrow money and "a death side" to pay the beneficiaries.

The life side is the section that holds all of your payments each month and the side you borrow money from, the catch being that you have one year to pay the money back but if you choose not to pay the money back after one year the policy is still open and active. The beneficiaries will still be paid.

Let's say your monthly payment on the life insurance policy is $500 per month. Always pay more than your monthly payment, pay $1,500 per month, or more. You decide how much extra you will pay, but always pay extra. This is how the rich and wealthy do it.

The Star of Wealth

10

BUSINESS FUNDING

The most challenging part of starting a business is getting the money to start. Working a job and hustling to save money to start the business will take a lot longer and it is the slow way, the harder way. We call this "getting it out the mud" but this isn't the way you want to go. Most of these big businesses you see today didn't get it out the mud, they got the money to start the business from loans and grants! I will give you a list of ways to get money for your business and you should try all of them! Leave no stone unturned.

- Angel Investors
- Factoring Loans
- Credit Cards
- Crowdfunding
- Grants
- Incubator Funding
- Minority and Women
- Grants and Loans

- Venture Capital
- Private Equity
- Hedge Funds
- Credit Unions

Angel Investors

An angel investor is a person with a lot of money who gives money to startup businesses in exchange of ownership equity in the company. They will become your partner in the business. Have you ever watched the TV Show *Shark Tank*? Those people that host the show and give entrepreneurs money to grow their business would be an example of angel investors and what they do. Three websites to find angel investors are:

- www.angelinvestmentnetwork.us
- www.angelcapitalassociation.org
- www.angellist.com.

There are many more ways to find angel investors, just Google search "angel investors" and explore your options.

Factoring Loans

These types of loans are used when you are already in business and need a loan. These loans are based on invoices from your customers that show you have money coming to you in the near future, to repay the loan. Let's say you have or own a trucking business and most of your big customers/clients pay you every 30 days. They give you invoices showing when the money they owe you will be put into your account. What you do is take all of your invoices to a lender that does "factor loans". After they review all of your invoices, they will decide how much they can lend you based on the amount of your invoices. Google search "factor loan lenders" in your city and state.

Credit Cards

A credit card is a card with money on it from a bank, credit union, financial lending institution, store or business. To get a credit card you will need a good personal credit score and credit history. You can get more money in the name of your business than you will get in your personal name. When you apply for business credit cards they will ask, "How much money has your business made in the last 12 months to 2 years?" Never ever put $0, always put what you want your business to make. The goal is to get as many business credit cards as you can. Run the money bag up!

Crowdfunding

Crowdfunding is the practice of funding a project or business by raising many small amounts of money from a lot of different people. Have you ever heard of GoFundMe? GoFundMe is popular for people raising money for bad situations that have fallen upon them, but this is an example of crowdfunding. Below are a few of the most popular crowdfunding platforms today:

Kickstarter

Kickstarter is a reward-based fundraiser platform. Backers (investors) are offered incentives to support you. Incentives like T-shirts, shoutouts, or exclusive pre-order discounts. You have to reach your funding goal in order to receive the money, if you do not reach your goal the money goes back to the people who donated it to you. For example, if your goal is to raise $50,000 you have to raise $50,000. If you only recieve $40,000 the money goes back to the people who put the money in the fund account.

Indiegogo (In-Dee-Go-Go)

Indiegogo is a strong crowdfunding platform that supports businesses, artists, and nonprofit organizations. On the Indiegogo platform you will be given the option to choose "a Fixed Funding goal" or a "Flexible Funding goal". Pick the Flexible Funding goal because if you do not raise all of the money you tried to raise you still will recieve the money. Ask and you shall receive.

PatreonPatreon focuses on funding for the new wave of hustlers/ entrepreneurs like bloggers, YouTubers, podcasters, cartoonists, musicians and live streamers. Patreon was made for creators and internet personalities with loyal audiences to generate recurring revenue (money) through paid memberships. Ask and you shall receive!

Crowdfunder/Shopify

Crowdfunder is a money raising platform that you use through the Shopify online app. Download the Shopify app on your phone and sign up in the Crowdfunder section of the app.

GoFundMe

GoFundMe is also a crowdfunding website that you can use to raise money for your new business. You will have to post it on all social media platforms where it can be seen by the people.

Fundable

Fundable allows new businesses to raise money by offering rewards or equity (ownership like the stock market) in their company in exchange for money. Google search "www.startups.com" to apply.

Seed Invest

Seed Invest is an equity crowdfunding platform where the people who give you money become part owners in your company after they pay you. Ps: When you are selling equity in your company you keep 51% of equity and sell the rest. 51% will keep you in power over your company and the majority shareholder.

Grants

A grant is money from an organization that you do not have to give the money. There are a lot of different businesses and organizations that give grants. First, apply for the government grants. There are three levels of grants from the government: federal grants, state grants and local grants. Logon to www.grants.gov and find the SBA grant section. SBA stands for Small Business Administration and apply for the grants available.

There are a lot of grants available, but you will have to dig, search and find them. See this is the stuff that the powers that be will not put on TV for everyone to see. They don't want you to know and that is the reason for this book! Google search "grants for business owners" and apply to every one you can find. No stone unturned.

Incubator Funding

Incubators are organizations that help companies that are just starting. Services provided by incubators include office space, administrative functions, education, mentorship and also connections to investors and money. Google search "incubator firms" in your city, then search the entire USA. No stone unturned!

Minority/Women-Owned Business Enterprises (MWBE)

The MWBE is an organization that provides help to minority and women owned businesses. You will need to go onto the website and apply for their certification first. After you receive the Certification there are countless benefits available for your business. Loans and grants are two of the ways they help you out. Gaining federal and state government contracts is the main benefit of this organization.

Venture Capital

Venture capital is used to help new businesses that have the potential to grow into big companies quickly. Venture capital firms raise money from Limited Partners (LP's). There are over 1,000 active venture capital firms in the USA. Google search "venture capital firms" and apply to all of them. Seek and you will find. No stone unturned.

Private Equity

Private equity firms invest money into new companies and create value. Usually when a private equity firm buys into a startup (new) company they might develop the products and services of the company. There are 14,089 private equity, hedge funds and investment vehicle businesses in the USA as of today. Google search "private equity firms" and find those that will help you. Ask and you shall receive, seek and you will find. No stone unturned!

Credit Unions

Credit unions are more business friendly and helpful to businesses. Credit unions are for the people; banks are for the money. Remember when you apply to banks and credit unions you need good personal credit which is why I put credit building in the very beginning of this book, because it is very important on this journey and will make your journey a lot easier. OPM other people's money is the name of the game that the rich play. Google search "credit unions" near you and apply to them first.

Hedge Funds

A hedge fund is a limited partnership of private investors whose money is managed by professional fund managers. For example, let's say all of the NFL players put their money together and let a manager make investments for them. Hedge funds are one of the most important sources of money for startup (new) companies. They provide the money that young companies need to grow their business. Hedge funds like to invest into new companies because of their high potential for growth and big profits. Google search "Hedge funds" and a lot of them will pop up. You Know the motto - No stone unturned. Seek and you will find.

OPERATION H.O.P.E.

Operation H.O.P.E. is a program that provides money coaches, who teach you what you need to know about business, coach you through the process and connect you to the resources you need to get it going and keep it going. Below are some of the services that Operation H.O.P.E. provide:

- Credit and Money Management
- Home Ownership
- Small Business Development
- Grant Opportunities
- Youth Programs

11

MOTIVATION & INSPIRATION

This is the way to freedom. When I say freedom, I mean the freedom of doing what you choose to do with your time—buying your time back. Time is your greatest asset, once it is gone you can never get it back. The freedom to wake up when you want, the freedom to take a vacation when you want to, without having to ask permission from an employer. The freedom of spending more time with those that you love and love you. The freedom of missing days of work without being fired.

On this side of the table you have control of your future; as a worker for someone else's company, they are in control. You have the power to set your own schedule as your own boss. As an employee the company you work for decides what time you come to work and what time you leave work. If you break the company's rules you will be punished in some way. When you are your own boss, you have the power to put people in positions to succeed, you have the power to give your family and friends jobs. As an entrepreneur you have the power to pass down a business to your kids. Most importantly, you have the power over your own life and time.

As an investor, and an entrepreneur, there are no limits. You can make as much money as you desire in a day's time. You are in a position where you can make a million dollars in one day! Trading your time for money as an employee, you will never see a million-dollar day. See, jobs have what you call a wage ceiling. A wage ceiling is a limit to how much you will be paid. You will only be paid as much as they want to pay you. If you walk around your house, stop, lean your head back and look up at the ceiling, that ceiling is the highest that you can rise up and that is how a job operates, with wage ceilings. Now take a look out of your bedroom window or take a walk outside and look up into the sky. That is your life as an entrepreneur/investor. A life of endless opportunity and no financial ceilings. As your own boss, the sky is the limit, and the sky is your life. No Limit!

All states in the USA except Montana are At-Will work states. At-Will means that any worker/employee can be fired for any reason, and without warning as long as the reason is not illegal. People like to use the phrase "job security", but what security is there when the law says that an employee can be fired for any reason.

The government has set a life plan for employees. The plan for an employee is to work until you reach 67 years old and start working at the age of 16. Therefore an employee has to work 51 years before they can retire. If you do not find a way to make money while you sleep, you will work until you die. If you ever have to work a job, which I pray that you never will, I want you to ask yourself these three questions:

1. Can I do this for 40-50 years?

2. Can I see myself doing this for the next 40-50 years?

3. Would I do this for 8-12 hours a day, for free?

If you answer no to any of these questions you shouldn't be there. You are not walking in your passion. You are not walking in your purpose.

The problem is the information given at school is not entrepreneur information. If you can change your information, you can change your destination. If you can change what's put in your mind, you can change the direction of your life. You can do anything you set your mind to; you were born to be great and to do big things. You were born to be the boss of your own financial future. You can do this, I know you can. Believe and receive, believe and achieve. The human mind can achieve anything, because everything is in it—the present, the past and the future.

The Federal Reserve prints 543 million dollars a day on a machine. They hold in storage 70-90 billion dollars. Therefore, there is no shortage of money, so never settle for less! Never give in and never give up; the sky is the limit and no weapon formed against you shall prosper.

12

CHOOSE A BUSINESS

When students go off to college for job training, they are given a book by the name of "The College Board Book of Majors". In this book are over 800 different job careers. Almost every job you can think of. When students are given this book, they will require you to pick a major, which is a job training program. Well, today I am telling you to pick a business to build or pick a business to buy. In this chapter, I will also teach you how to choose a business as well as the most important things to analyze before you choose a business to build or buy.

SHAREHOLDER

When you buy businesses through the stock market you become a shareholder. A shareholder is a person or business that owns a business by buying shares in that company. As a shareholder you invest money into a business that is already up and running. In return, you receive money from that business. You are not involved with running the business! You are trading money for money!

Power of a Shareholder

Depending on the shareholder agreement and the rules of the companies that you buy, a shareholder has the power to:

- Sell their shares
- Receive dividend payments
- Gain access to company financial information
- Purchase new shares issued by the company
- Sue the company for violation of fiduciary duty (a fiduciary is someone that manages money or property for someone else.)
- Vote on the directors of the company
- Propose shareholder resolutions
- Attend company annual meetings

S&P 500

S&P stands for Standard and Poor's. The S&P 500 is a stock market index tracking the stock performance of 500 of the largest companies listed on the stock exchanges in the United States.

This is where you will make your first investment in the stock market. You cannot invest directly in the S&P 500, therefore you will invest in other index funds that own all of the companies that are listed on the S&P 500.

When you buy shares of this index fund, you indirectly own all 500 companies within the index fund, and you are in position to receive benefits from all 500 companies.

3 INDEX FUNDS THAT MIRROR THE S&P 500 INDEX FUND

1. Vanguard 500 Index Fund Admiral (VFIAX)

2. Schwab S&P 500 Index Fund Select (SWPPX)

3. Fidelity 500 Index Fund (FXAIX)

1. Vanguard 500 Index Fund Admiral

- $3,000 initial investment (down payment)
- $387.66 share price (as of today)
- $820.72 billion net assets

2. Schwab S&P 500 Index Fund Select

- $0 initial investment (down payment)
- $64.59 share price (as of today)
- $67 billion net assets

3. Fidelity 500 Index Fund

- $0 initial investment (down payment)
- $145.79 share price (as of today)
- $388 billion net assets

Choose any of these three to get started. After your brokerage account is set up, simply call your brokerage company and speak with a representative and they will walk you through the process.

Why Should You Invest in Index Funds First?

The main reason for investing in the indices that mirror the S&P 500 is because it almost guarantees that you will win the game of investing!

A Lifetime Commitment

When you buy into the index fund, this is a lifetime commitment, just like a marriage! Until death do you part. Once you are in forever, do not take any money out and do not sell your shares. Compound interest will be a great blessing to your financial future!

COMPANIES INSIDE OF THE INDICES (INDEX)

1. Apple

2. Microsoft

3. Amazon

4. Nvidia

5. Tesla

6. Berkshire Hathaway

7. Exxon Mobil

8. United Health Group

9. Facebook

10. Google

11. Johnson + Johnson

12. Chase Bank

13. Visa

14. MasterCard

15. Home Depot

16. Chevron

17. McDonald's

18. Costco

19. Coca-Cola

20. Pepsi

21. Walmart

22. Bank of America

23. Walt Disney

24. Comcast

25. NikeVerizon

26. Netflix

27. Starbucks

These are only 28 of the 503 company stocks that are in the index fund, which means that you will indirectly own all of these great companies. To see all 500+ companies, Google search the index fund.

BUYING INDIVIDUAL COMPANIES (STOCK)

Before You Buy Shares of a Company

As an investor your job is to do research on a company before you buy it. No one can do this for you—homework is mandatory!

The ultimate goal is to buy great profitable businesses at a fair or discounted price!! Companies that will be around a long time, 50-100 years. You want to invest in the companies that will feed your family forever!

Getting to Know a Company

You want to learn about the company just like you learn about a person. Get to know a company, just like you get to know a person.

When first getting to know the company, don't look at the money, we will do that after we get to know the company personally. Only invest in businesses that are in your circle of competence/companies that you understand!

Just like a person, you want to know when the company was born, its birthday. You want to know how old the company is and how long it has been in business.

Find out who the parents of the company are; we would call the Founder and the CEO the parent. Is the CEO a good CEO? How does he run the company? Does he own any shares in the company? What are his viewpoints for the company? What are his projected plans for the company?

What product or service does the company sell? What does the world think about their product or service? How does the company sell its product or service? Does the company have a competitive moat? A moat is a company's competitive advantage that protects them from their competition.

Moat Explained

A moat is like a special skill or special power that makes the company great. A moat is something that other companies cannot copy! Think about the great Michael Jordan: What was his moat? What made Michael Jordan the best basketball player during his time? Stephen Curry the great 3-Point shooter that plays for the Golden State Warriors, what is his moat? Apple, the creator of the iPhone is said to be the greatest company in the history of the US. But, what is Apple's moat? What makes Apple the best? There are cellphones everywhere, so what makes the iPhone the best? Can someone create a phone just like the iPhone or better? When researching a company you must find out if they have a moat, and if they do, find out what it is.

Get to Know the Financial Business

After you learn the personal things about the business you want to buy, the next step is to dig into their money business. Just because a company has been alive a long time does not mean they have been profitable (making big money) a long time. You have to dig into their money records. You want to know about the company's past history and their up-to-date present!

Just like knowing your spouse's financial situation, you want to know the business's financial health. How much money does the company have in its savings account? How much debt does the company have? What is the company's net worth? How much money does the business make every 3 months (quarterly)? What are the company's quarterly expenses?

Quarterly Reports

Most employees/workers get a paycheck every week. On the paycheck is how many hours they have worked and how much they have been paid for that particular week and how much they have been paid for the year. It also shows how much money has been taken out (expenses) of their pay for the week and year. Therefore, if you wanted to know how much money a person is making, take a look at their paycheck stub.

A Quarterly Report is just like a paycheck. It will show you how much money a company is making every 3 months and how much money is being taken out (expenses) every 3 months. There are four quarters in a year. When you look at a company's investor page you may see Q1, Q2 Q3, or Q4. Those abbreviations are short for Quarter 1, Quarter 2, Quarter 3 and Quarter 4.

Financial Statements

Financial statements are written records that show the money activities and the money (financial) performance of a company. This is where you find out what you need to know! Financial statements include the balance sheet, income statement,

statement of cash flow and statement of changes in equity.

1. <u>Balance sheet</u>: When you look at a balance sheet, focus on <u>current assets/current liabilities</u>. Then look at <u>total assets/ total liabilities</u>. Current assets subtract <u>current liabilities</u> equal: working capital. You want the working capital of the company you are buying to be positive. Working capital (money) is used to fund operations and meet short-term obligations. A lot of businesses that have gone bankrupt had negative working capital.

2. <u>Income statement</u>: When you look at an income statement, focus on the <u>top line</u> which is revenue (sales) and the <u>bottom line</u> which is profit. <u>Cost of Revenue</u> is what the company has paid to bring in the sales, which is marketing, advertising and all other tactics a company has used to bring in sales.

3. <u>Cash Flow Statement:</u> Cash Flow is the money going in and out of a business; you want this to be positive. If the business is not investing money correctly, if the business isn't loaning money properly, or if the business is not investing shareholder money right (which is your money), then it will be negative. There is a metric that we look at that is called ROIC (Return on Invested Capital), and this information is recorded on the cash flow statement. A cash flow statement allows investors to understand how a company's operations are running, where its money is coming from and how money is being spent.

Annual Report

An annual report is a report on a company's activities throughout the past year. Annual reports are intended to give shareholders and other interested people information about the company's activities and money performance. Typical annual reports may include:

- General corporate information
- Operating and financial review
- Directors' report
- Corporate governance information
- Chairperson's statement
- Auditor's Report
- Sustainability and ESG information
- Contents: non-audited information
- Financial statements including: Balance SheetIncome Statement

    A. Statement of Changes in Equity
    B. Cash Flow Statement
    C. Notes to the Financial Statements
    D. Accounting Policies
    E. Independent Assurance Statements
    F. Other Features

The details in the report are for investors to understand the useful company's money position and future direction.

Form 10-K

A Form 10-K is an annual report required by the United States Securities and Exchange Commission (SEC) that gives a complete summary of a company's money performance. The 10-K includes information such as:

A. A Company's History
B. Organization Structure– how operations are directed to meet a company's objectives and goals.
C. Executive Compensation– is made up of both the financial compensation (money) and other non-financial benefits, received by executives (senior managers).
D. Equity

E. Subsidiaries– other companies owned by the parent company.

F. Audited Financial Statements– Financial statements that have been examined, inspected, and verified.

Annual General Meeting

Every state requires public companies to hold an annual general meeting of shareholders to elect the Board of Directors and transact other business that requires shareholder approval. All public companies are required to make their annual meeting materials available online.

At this meeting, the shareholders and partners may receive copies of the company's accounts, review of fiscal information for the past year and ask questions regarding the directions the business will take in the future.

P/E Ratio

P/E Ratio is short for price-earnings ratio. The ratio is used for valuing companies and to find out if the company is overvalued or undervalued.

P/E Ratio Formula

The P/E ratio formula is:

What this means is that it would take 8 years to make your money back if the cost of the share was $24 and the company paid you $3 per year. As you know, when you are paid in dividends, you are paid based on the share price. You are paid a percentage (dividend yield) of the share price.

52-Week High

52-week high is a phrase that is used to let investors know what a stock/share is at its most expensive price;. Do not buy at this time; wait until it goes down to a fair or discounted price.

Never buy a company when the share price is at its 52-week high.

52-Week Range

When you are researching a company, you will see a section on their financial charts that says 52-Week Range. There are 52 weeks in one year, and within 52 weeks a share is sold at different prices. The 52-week range system records all of the prices that a share of a company has sold at. The 52-week range system then lets investors know the lowest price a share has sold at, the highest price a share has sold at, and the current price of the share. Moreover, the 52-week range graph images shows if the current share price is at a low or high point.

52-Week Range Chart

The 52-Week range chart is simple and easy to read and understand. This is how one may look on a company's financial profile page:

52-Week Range:

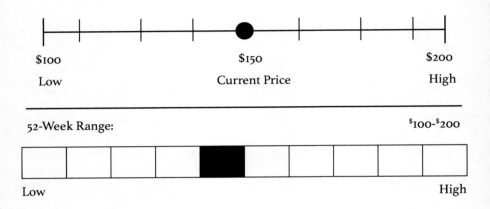

The black shaded box would show the current price, which would be about $150.

When to Buy a Stock/Share

When buying great companies it's all about timing. Remember the motto "buy great companies at fair or discount prices". The secret of business is to buy a great business at the right time. Buy a great company just like people shop for clothes and shoes. Wait until there is a sale! Wait until the share price drops! Once again, buy great companies at discount prices!

Dividend History

When researching a company look at their dividend payment history. Call it a dividend background check. What you are looking for is if the company has increased their dividend payments in the last 5-10 years. No human can predict the future, but in this business, investors use or try to use the past history to predict the future. With that being said, if the company has increased how much they pay investors in the past, they may continue this habit of paying the investors more. When companies stop paying dividends, this is a bad sign that they might be going through money problems, so pay attention to the company's moves.

Bull Market and Bear Market

These are terms that you will hear often, and you need to know what they are and what they mean. When you hear someone say the stock market is in a <u>Bull Market</u> that simply means that the price of assets (stocks) have gone up (increased). The term <u>Bear Market</u> means that the price of assets (stocks) have gone down (decreased).

You need to be aware of where the market is, if it is in a bull market or bear market.

Ticker Symbols

Ticker symbols are like nicknames. For the company, you will hear the phrase ticker symbol often. Allow me to show you some company ticker symbols.

Company Name	Ticker Symbol
Apple	AAPL
Amazon	AMZN
Microsoft	MSFT
Starbucks	SBUX
Chipotle	CMG

Buy and Hold

Buy and hold means that you plan on keeping the asset/stock for the long run. Some people or investors are only in the game to make quick money for the moment. True wealth is built over time, in the long run. Again, you want to buy great companies at a discount share price and own the stocks/ companies for a lifetime.

Invest with No Emotions

We all as humans have an emotional attachment and relationship with money. We are happy, excited, joyful, generous, loving, merry, jovial and content when the money is coming to us in the amount that we desire. On the flip side, when we lose money or money isn't coming in as we would like it to, we tend to allow negative emotions to consume us—emotions like fear, sadness, depression, anger, frustration, hopelessness, anxiety, disgust, shame, annoyance, disappointment and hurt.

In business and investing, do not allow your emotions to control when you buy or sell a company (stock/shares). The thing is that the stock market goes up and down by the minute. You may look at your account in the morning and see that you have made $1,000 before lunch time, then check it at 3pm and see you have lost $600. The stock market is like a bipolar friend that just cannot stay consistent. Therefore, when you see that you are losing do not allow fear to force you to sell your great company. This business of stock market investing was created by powerful people and was designed to keep powerful people rich and wealthy. Therefore, the stock market as a whole may go down but it will always go back up! Act off intelligence and information, not emotions! When a stock goes down don't be fearful; when a stock goes up, don't be excited.

Feed Your Brokerage Account

Treat your businesses and brokerage accounts as if it was a baby, well it is a baby, your baby. Therefore, you have to feed it to keep it growing. Put money in your account as often as you can, whether it be daily, every other day, weekly, bi-weekly, or monthly. It's up to you to decide how often you feed your account money, but you must feed it regularly.

During the time you are waiting patiently for a company's stock price to go down, you want the money to be close and on hand so you can buy quickly.

Feed your account!

Where to Find Company Records

There are many different websites available to do homework on a company. The best way to find financial records is to go to the investor relations section of the company website or log on to www. sec.gov.

Study the Greats

Study the greats and become greater! Two greats of this stock market investing game are Peter Lynch and Warren Buffett.

Peter Lynch is an American investor that is famous for turning 18 million dollars into 14 billion dollars in only 13 years. You can learn a lot about buying businesses from Peter, just Google search his name and the books about stock market investing that he has written will appear. I suggest that you start reading them now.

Warren Buffett is respected by many as being the G-O-A-T (greatest of all time) of investing. As of today Warren Buffett is 92 years old, he bought his first company through the stock market at the age of 11! Therefore, you can say he has 81 years of experience in the game of growing money. As of today, May 17, 2023, he is worth $114 billion dollars! His company Berkshire Hathaway is worth $723 billion dollars!

Though Warren has never in his life worked a physically hard day at a job, he has worked the most powerful muscle that God has given us, the brain! Buffett says that he reads 5,000 pages per day! That could mean that he reads 2-3 books per day, every day. Are you willing to put in that much work to reach your goals?

Warren Buffett owns about 50 different stocks (companies) through the stock market. You can learn a lot about the game of businesses from Buffett.

Books to Read

More knowledge, more power! As I told you earlier, Buffett reads 5,000 pages a day! There is an old saying that says: "If want to hide something from a nigger, put you it in a book". You must self-educate yourself daily, put the phones up, put away the iPads and read books about business ownership. Below are some books you need to read:

1. *The Intelligent Investor*: By Benjamin Graham

2. *One Up on Wall Street*: By Peter Lynch

3. *Learn to Earn*: By Peter Lynch

4. *The Warren Buffett Way*: By Robert G. Hagstrom

5. *Common Sense on Mutual Funds*: By John Bogle

Last but not least, Google search "the wall street trapper" and enroll in his college at www.thetrapperuniversity.com

CHOOSE A FRANCHISE

The World is Yours and Every Great Business in it!

In this section, I will be showing you some of the top performing franchise opportunities in the USA.

1. Buffalo Wild Wings Franchise

   Cost: $564,100 - $4,604,800

   Gross Revenue per year: $950,000 - $3.1 million (average)

   (How much you make))
   _____

2. Jimmy John's Franchise

   Cost: $355, 900 - $671,400

   Gross Revenue per year : $900,000 (average)

   (How much you make)
   _____

3. Valvoline Instant Oil Change Franchise

   Cost: $204,750 - $3.3 million

   Gross Revenue Per Year: $175,000 - $2.6 million (average)

   (How much you make)
   _____

4. Steak' N Shake Franchise

Cost: $155,970 - $1.7 million

Gross Revenue per year: $1.6 million (average)

(How much you make)

5. KFC Restaurant Franchise

Cost: $1.4 million - $3.2 million

Gross Revenue per year : $1.34 million (average)

6. McDonald's Franchise

Cost: $1.36 million - $2.45 million

Gross Revenue per year: $3.4 million (average)

7. Arby's Restaurant Franchise

Cost: $628, 950 - $2.3 million

Gross Revenue per year: $1.3 million (average)

8. Planet Fitness Gym Franchise

Cost: $1.6 million - $4.9 million

Gross Revenue Per Year: $1.6 million (average)

9. U.P.S. Store Franchise

Cost: $185,306 - $474,193

Gross Revenue Per Year: $607,750 (average)

10. Burger King Restaurant Franchise

Cost: $230,000 - $4,194,700

Gross Revenue Per Year: $1.2 - $1.4 million (average)

11. Baskin-Robbins Ice Cream Store Franchise

Cost: $91,000 - $625,000

Gross Revenue Per Year: $420,000 - $1.4 million (average)

12. Taco Bell Franchise

Cost: $1.3 million - $3.4 million

Gross Revenue Per Year: $1.6 million (average)

13. Subway Franchise

Cost: $167, 600 - $477,000

Gross Revenue Per Year: $400,000 (average)

14. Texas Roadhouse Restaurant Franchise

Cost: $2.1 million - $6.5 million

Gross Revenue Per Year: $3.8 million (average)

15. Wing Stop Franchise

Cost: $348,000 - $760,000

Gross Revenue Per Year: $1.5 million (average)

16. Popeyes Restaurant Franchise

Cost: $424,000 - $2.7 million

Gross Revenue Per Year: $1.7 million (average)

17. Smoothie King Franchise

Cost: $260,000 - $850,000

Gross Revenue Per Year: $600,000 - $850,000 (average)

18. Dunkin' Donuts Franchise

Cost: $98,000 - $1.7 million (average)

Gross Revenue Per Year: $620,000 - $1.3 million (average)

There are lots of franchisee opportunities in America, this is only some of them. You can pick one of these or you can Google search "franchise opportunities" to find different ones. You can do anything you set your mind to. Think big, dream big and do it big!

PICK A BUSINESS TO BUILD (LLC)

Before You Commit to a Business

Before you fully commit to a business to build there are a few important things you need to think about before you file your LLC paperwork. Those 8 most important things are:

1. Work

2. Risk

3. Knowledge

4. Problem Solving

5. Longevity

6. Moats

7. Why

8. Demand

1. Work : What work will I have to put in this business?

This is probably the most important thing, choosing any business to build because in the beginning you may have to work in your business doing a lot of different task on your own. The goal is to put the business in a position where it can be run without you, but in the beginning the business will need you, so be prepared to grind, and grind consistently until you can step back and let the business run without you.

During this phase and stage of the business building process you will learn a whole lot, it's like training camp for bosses, where you get hands-on experience of building your business. You need to know what kind of work each business will require because if you start the business and later find out that you do not enjoy doing the work, chances are that you will stop putting in the work. If you do not like or love the work that will be required, do not start the business! There will be some tasks that you will enjoy doing and there will be some tasks that you absolutely hate doing depending on the business that you want to build. Therefore, if the bad outweighs the good, choose a different business. Be prepared mentally to put in a lot of hours, sometimes more than you would at a job. But let me tell you this, "You would rather wear your own company uniform to work, than wearing somebody else's company uniform to work".

Example of the Work:

- Tree Cutting Business.

  A. May have to work in the hot sun
  B. May have to climb trees
  C. May have to take a class on tree cutting
  D. May have to work long hours
  E. May have to manage people

Once you look inside the business, you can see what work you will have to put in, then you will be able to decide if you are willing to do the work. If you are willing to do the work, start the business!

2. Risk - What are the risks of the business?

The risk of a business are the things that you could lose by involving yourself in a business. In any and every business there are two main risks that are present. Those two risks are time and money. Have no fear, money can be gotten again if lost. Time, you can't get back, but you will learn a lot on your journey that will make up for the feeling of time being lost. Most people think that if they did not make as much money as they wanted to that they have completely lost out, but they overlook and underestimate the knowledge and experience that they have gained during the process of running and building a business. Big money, real money is always the goal, but money is not the only prize that you win on the journey! Each business will have different risks that come with the business, and you need to find those risks, then decide if you are willing to take those risks!

Example of the Business Risks:

- Tree Cutting Business

  A. Could lose money
  B. Could lose time
  C. Could fall out of a tree
  D. Could cut myself with the chainsaw

After you find the risks, think of ways to eliminate them if possible.

3. Knowledge - What knowledge do I need to run this business?

With any service or product that you choose to sell you need to know everything about that product or service. Customers will ask you a million questions about what you are selling to learn about the product or service and to see if you know about what you are trying to sell to them. Customers have a fear of losing money, and you can ease this fear by letting them know that you know about your product or service. You also need to know your product or service in order to teach it to your employees. You may need to take some classes or read some books or maybe even get a job doing what you plan to do within your business to get some hands-on experience. Whatever it takes to get the knowledge you need, do it! Get the knowledge by any means necessary!

Example of Gaining Knowledge:

- Tree Cutting Business

    A. May have to read some books on management
    B. May have to go to school for tree cutting
    C. May have to get a job cutting trees for a few months

4. Problem Solving - What problem will I be solving for people?

ALL businesses should solve a problem for consumers and so should yours.

Example of the Problem:

- Tree Cutting Business

  A. Preventing trees from falling on houses and damaging property by cutting them down.

5. Longevity - How long can this business last?

The goal is always to own businesses that will last until the world ends even though some business opportunities will be short lived, it's just the nature of business. Businesses are born and businesses die, that's the risk of business. The question is how long the business can live. Even the best of the best have experienced the early death of a business they have owned in their career, it's all part of the game. Study your business industry

and try to see into the future to somewhat predict
how long your business can last.

Example of Longevity:

- Tree Cutting Business

    A. I think the business can last forever
       because trees will always grow and need
       to be cut down for different reasons.
    B. Trees will need to be cut before new real
       estate is built.
    C. Hurricanes and tornadoes come every
       year and knock down trees, therefore they
       will need to be cut and removed.

6. Moats - What will be my moat?

Most likely there will be other businesses already
doing what you want to do, therefore, you will
need a moat to put you ahead of the other
businesses. What will make your business better
than the other businesses? What will you do that
they will not be able to do? What will be your

superhero business power that other companies cannot copy? They might do it, but make sure they can't do it like you!!

Example of a Company Moat:

- Tree Cutting Business

    A. I will invent a machine that cuts 300-foot-tall trees in 5 seconds and charge a cheaper price than everybody in the world.

7. Why - Why do I want this business?

Get a sheet of paper and write out all of the reasons why you want to own the business.

You need to see your reasons on paper for why you want the business. If your reasons are good reasons that make sense, move forward and start the business building process.
Examples of Why:

- Tree Cutting Business

A. I like to cut trees

B. I can give my family and friends a jobI can set my own schedule

C. I can take vacations whenever I want to

D. The tree cutting business is in high demand

E. I want to help people during hurricane season

F. I like being outside

8. Demand - Is there a demand for the product or service I want to sell?

Do people desire what you are planning to sell? You want to sell products and services that consumers want and need! If the product or service does not have a demand, people will not spend money with you. If you give people what they want, they will give you what you want, the money!

Example of Demand:

• Tree Cutting Business

A. From June 1st to November 30th is hurricane season; during this time people will need trees cut down, and the demand for tree cutting services will be high.

You can sell any product or service you choose! But here are a few businesses that you can start right in your neighborhood.

B. Selling Candy - World famous chocolate
C. Garage Sales - Sell your old shoes and clothes
D. Car Washing Business - Washing cars
E. Lawn Care Business - Cutting grassVending Machines - Soda and candy machines

This is only the beginning of your journey. During this phase you will learn things about business that will be with you a lifetime. Get started and be great!

Apple Inc.
CONDENSED CONSOLIDATED STATEMENTS OF OPERATIONS (Unaudited)
(In millions, except number of shares which are reflected in thousands and per share amounts)

	Three Months Ended		Six Months Ended	
	April 1, 2023	March 26, 2022	April 1, 2023	March 26, 2022
Net sales:				
Products	$ 73,929	$ 77,457	$ 170,317	$ 181,886
Services	20,907	19,821	41,673	39,337
Total net sales [(1)]	94,836	97,278	211,990	221,223
Cost of sales:				
Products	46,795	49,290	107,560	113,599
Services	6,065	5,429	12,122	10,822
Total cost of sales	52,860	54,719	119,682	124,421
Gross margin	41,976	42,559	92,308	96,802
Operating expenses:				
Research and development	7,457	6,387	15,166	12,693
Selling, general and administrative	6,201	6,193	12,808	12,642
Total operating expenses	13,658	12,580	27,974	25,335
Operating income	28,318	29,979	64,334	71,467
Other income/(expense), net	64	160	(329)	(87)
Income before provision for income taxes	28,382	30,139	64,005	71,380
Provision for income taxes	4,222	5,129	9,847	11,740
Net income	$ 24,160	$ 25,010	$ 54,158	$ 59,640
Earnings per share:				
Basic	$ 1.53	$ 1.54	$ 3.42	$ 3.65
Diluted	$ 1.52	$ 1.52	$ 3.41	$ 3.62
Shares used in computing earnings per share:				
Basic	15,787,154	16,278,802	15,839,939	16,335,263
Diluted	15,847,050	16,403,316	15,901,384	16,461,304
[(1)] Net sales by reportable segment:				
Americas	$ 37,784	$ 40,882	$ 87,062	$ 92,378
Europe	23,945	23,287	51,626	53,036
Greater China	17,812	18,343	41,717	44,126
Japan	7,176	7,724	13,931	14,831
Rest of Asia Pacific	8,119	7,042	17,654	16,852
Total net sales	$ 94,836	$ 97,278	$ 211,990	$ 221,223
[(1)] Net sales by category:				
iPhone	$ 51,334	$ 50,570	$ 117,109	$ 122,198
Mac	7,168	10,435	14,903	21,287
iPad	6,670	7,646	16,066	14,894
Wearables, Home and Accessories	8,757	8,806	22,239	23,507
Services	20,907	19,821	41,673	39,337
Total net sales	$ 94,836	$ 97,278	$ 211,990	$ 221,223

Apple Inc.

CONDENSED CONSOLIDATED BALANCE SHEETS (Unaudited)
(In millions, except number of shares which are reflected in thousands and par value)

	April 1, 2023	September 24, 2022
ASSETS:		
Current assets:		
Cash and cash equivalents	$ 24,687	$ 23,646
Marketable securities	31,185	24,658
Accounts receivable, net	17,936	28,184
Inventories	7,482	4,946
Vendor non-trade receivables	17,963	32,748
Other current assets	13,660	21,223
Total current assets	112,913	135,405
Non-current assets:		
Marketable securities	110,461	120,805
Property, plant and equipment, net	43,398	42,117
Other non-current assets	65,388	54,428
Total non-current assets	219,247	217,350
Total assets	$ 332,160	$ 352,755
LIABILITIES AND SHAREHOLDERS' EQUITY:		
Current liabilities:		
Accounts payable	$ 42,945	$ 64,115
Other current liabilities	56,425	60,845
Deferred revenue	8,131	7,912
Commercial paper	1,996	9,982
Term debt	10,578	11,128
Total current liabilities	120,075	153,982
Non-current liabilities:		
Term debt	97,041	98,959
Other non-current liabilities	52,886	49,142
Total non-current liabilities	149,927	148,101
Total liabilities	270,002	302,083
Commitments and contingencies		
Shareholders' equity:		
Common stock and additional paid-in capital, $0.00001 par value: 50,400,000 shares authorized; 15,723,406 and 15,943,425 shares issued and outstanding, respectively	69,568	64,849
Retained earnings/(Accumulated deficit)	4,336	(3,068)
Accumulated other comprehensive income/(loss)	(11,746)	(11,109)
Total shareholders' equity	62,158	50,672
Total liabilities and shareholders' equity	$ 332,160	$ 352,755

Apple Inc.

CONDENSED CONSOLIDATED STATEMENTS OF CASH FLOWS (Unaudited)
(In millions)

	Six Months Ended	
	April 1, 2023	March 26, 2022
Cash, cash equivalents and restricted cash, beginning balances	$ 24,977	$ 35,929
Operating activities:		
Net income	54,158	59,640
Adjustments to reconcile net income to cash generated by operating activities:		
Depreciation and amortization	5,814	5,434
Share-based compensation expense	5,591	4,517
Other	(1,732)	1,068
Changes in operating assets and liabilities:		
Accounts receivable, net	9,596	5,542
Inventories	(2,548)	1,065
Vendor non-trade receivables	14,785	643
Other current and non-current assets	(4,092)	(3,542)
Accounts payable	(20,764)	(1,750)
Other current and non-current liabilities	1,757	2,515
Cash generated by operating activities	62,565	75,132
Investing activities:		
Purchases of marketable securities	(11,197)	(61,987)
Proceeds from maturities of marketable securities	17,124	18,000
Proceeds from sales of marketable securities	1,897	24,668
Payments for acquisition of property, plant and equipment	(6,703)	(5,317)
Other	(247)	(735)
Cash generated by/(used in) investing activities	874	(25,371)
Financing activities:		
Payments for taxes related to net share settlement of equity awards	(2,734)	(3,218)
Payments for dividends and dividend equivalents	(7,418)	(7,327)
Repurchases of common stock	(39,069)	(43,109)
Repayments of term debt	(3,651)	(3,750)
Proceeds from/(Repayments of) commercial paper, net	(7,960)	999
Other	(455)	(105)
Cash used in financing activities	(61,287)	(56,510)
Increase/(Decrease) in cash, cash equivalents and restricted cash	2,152	(6,749)
Cash, cash equivalents and restricted cash, ending balances	$ 27,129	$ 29,180
Supplemental cash flow disclosure:		
Cash paid for income taxes, net	$ 4,894	$ 9,301
Cash paid for interest	$ 1,873	$ 1,406

13

THE ALPHABETS OF WEALTH

ASSETS

BANK

CREDIT

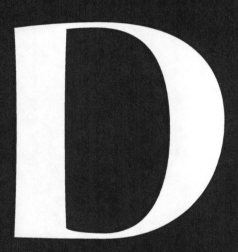

DEBIT

EQUITY

FINANCE

GRANTS

H

HELOC

I

INVEST

Joint Venture

Knowledge Capital

L

Liability

Marketing

Networking

Ownership

Private Lender

Qualitative Analysis

Return on Investment

Stocks & Shares

Trust Fund

Underwriter

Venture Capital

Wealth

Yield

Z

Zoning

14

SELF-AFFIRMATIONS

Every day you need to spend at least 30 minutes alone, just you and the oxygen (LOL). No phones, No iPads, no TVs, no TikTok, no Instagram, no Facebook. Eliminate all external distractions. It's time to tap into your powers of visualization. My people perish without a vision.

Just as the human mind can visualize bad things, the human mind can also visualize great things. Close your eyes and see yourself buying real estate, see yourself buying great businesses through the stock market, visualize the mansion you want to live in.

Repeat the Following Statements Out Loud to Yourself ⬇

- I will change my life one share at a time.
- I will create other bosses.
- I will invest my time in business owner education.

- I will manage my money properly.
- I will control the money, the money won't control me.
- I will make the money, the money won't make me.
- I will buy real estate at discounted prices.
- I will buy great companies at discounted prices.
- The sky is the limit.
- The secret to business is to buy a great business.
- I will learn how to build a business.
- I will learn how to scale a business.
- I have the burning desire to win.
- I will redesign my family's financial blueprint.
- I will change the way my family gets money.
- Money will work for me, and I will work for knowledge.
- I am great.

- I am my own boss.
- I am the owner of profitable businesses.
- I am the Chosen One.
- I am a conqueror.
- I am determined to win.
- I am destined to win.
- It's not over until I win.
- Nothing will stop my greatness.
- I will learn the game and earn from the game.
- I can learn anything.
- I am a learning machine.
- I am an employer not an employee.
- I am a business owner.
- I am the captain of my ship.
- I am the architect of my financial future.
- I am rich forever.
- I will not be denied.
- I am fearless.
- I am a calculated risk taker.

- I'm strong like King Kong.
- I will never settle for less.
- I will live a life of abundance.
- Money is not the root of evil.
- I am relentless.
- I am an investor.
- I will build a real estate portfolio.
- I will build a great credit history.
- I will build great business credit.
- I am the head and not the tail.
- I am a leader and not a follower.
- I will learn from the mistakes of others and not make those same mistakes on my journey.
- I will work to build my own business.
- I will be a billionaire.
- I'm a hustler not a customer.
- I am the owner of businesses, not a consumer of businesses.
- I will master the stock market.
- I will buy franchises.

- I will build a team.
- I will allocate capital.
- I am committed to owning assets.

In loving memory of Gregory Foster, Eleanor Leathers, Aaron Warren, Arthur Warren, Pamela Warren, Covadis Knighten Jr., Roosevelt Lane, and Leroy Ronnie Scott rest in heaven, see you when I get there.